POWER OF UNDERSTANDING

How Personality Influences Our Lives

RICK TOOMEY, Ed.D.

Jan-Carol
Publishing, Inc
"every story needs a book"

Power of Understanding
How Personality Influences Our Lives
Rick Toomey, Ed.D.

Published August 2022
Express Editions
Imprint of Jan-Carol Publishing, Inc.
All rights reserved
Copyright © 2022 Rick Toomey, Ed.D.

ISBN: 978-1-954978-57-7
Library of Congress Control Number: 2022944318

Jan-Carol Publishing, Inc.
PO Box 701
Johnson City, TN 37605
publisher@jancarolpublishing.com
www.jancarolpublishing.com

DEDICATION

The major influence in helping me in the practical use of MBTI was my dear friend and colleague Zellie Earnest. I observed him use it to help individuals and groups better understand themselves and others in a way that improved their lives at work and away from work. As internal organizational development consultants, we had the opportunity to utilize MBTI as a tool for improving individual, leadership, team, and organizational effectiveness for a Fortune 500 company and various groups in our community. This book would not have been written without Zellie's influence in my life and as a result it is dedicated to him and his memory.

As I was proofreading this book for the last time, I began Chapter 4 about the Extraversion/Introversion preference on MBTI by sharing about my son, Chris, being an Extravert and I used the phrase "he has multiple networks of friends." It has been a little over 10 weeks since Chris died of a heart attack. The response to his death by hundreds of people confirmed the stories I have shared in this book about his love for people and interacting with them. In addition to Zellie, I want to dedicate this book to Chris. He was and still is an inspiration to me and so many people. I have chosen to keep my stories about him in the present tense because in many ways he is still with us. Our family will be writing a book about Chris and friendship because he was so many people's best friend.

CONTENTS

FOREWORD

By Carol Cross

Early in my tenure as Vice President of Human Resources/Training and Development of Company B (whom you will hear more about in the text of this book), I was formally introduced to Rick Toomey by the President & CEO (my boss) of Company B. The purpose for this introduction was to discuss the organization's need for a customized leadership training program. Company B was originally formed as a credit union in 1934 serving employees of Company A (also mentioned in Dr. Toomey's book, *Power of Understanding*). In 2005, Company B separated from Company A and expanded to a community-chartered credit union opening membership to the wider community. We had left the "mother-ship" and were faced with providing our own internal resources for an employee base 100% focused on serving members. In the service world, every team member must function as a leader and being a great communicator is a key component for success.

Rick's doctoral education and more than 30 years of experience in psychology, counseling, and organizational development had led to successful engagements with other organizations, and he had a commendable reputation in the field of organizational, team, and leadership development. Rick also taught Organizational Development and Training at a local university. He simply was considered the best of the best by reputation and results, and we knew he was "our person" to advise, develop, and deliver a program to maximize our mission of developing strong leaders at all levels delivering the highest level of service to our members/customers.

During multiple meetings, the CEO, Rick, and I discussed the critical building blocks we envisioned. Since each of the three of us, had previous experience with the Myers-Briggs Type Indicator and recognized its value in helping to better understand both self and others, we quickly agreed this tool was a cornerstone for building and maintaining strong, effective relationships with both internal and external customers.

While our training focus was initially on managers at all levels of the organization, we soon realized the value of driving the knowledge and use of MBTI throughout the organization, top to bottom. We knew front-line staff are the face and voice of any service business and effective communication is critical. Every Company B employee is required to complete the foundational MBTI course as a part of their personal and interpersonal effectiveness training. Very quickly after implementation, we began to hear exciting stories from employees at all levels about how they had used this new tool not only to improve communication and service to customers and co-workers, but also how they utilized this knowledge to improve personal relationships with family, friends, and people in the community.

As a rapidly growing organization, our employee base increased by 10-15% per year over multiple years resulting in rapid internal movement and the formation of new and constantly changing teams. In addition to delivering a broad range of leadership training, Rick quickly became actively involved in evaluating the MBTI makeup of the larger organization, as well as individual departments, and teams. Through this process, Rick counseled and coached managers and teams throughout the organization to better understand one another and operate more effectively and efficiently together. It became evident that MBTI was becoming deeply imbedded into our culture, our thinking, our shared language, and common ground. MBTI influenced positive and successful strategic outcomes—one conversation, one interaction, one customer at a time. I am proud to say that Company B achieved and has maintained one of the highest customer experience ratings, not only in the financial industry but across multiple industries, year over year. In addition, Company B is highly regarded as one of the top performers in its field and is highly sought after as an employer of choice.

I can confidently say that "people don't care what you know until they know you care." We each show others every day how much we care by the way we listen, communicate, and how we treat them. In a very tough world that matters!

In his book, *Power of Understanding*, Rick breaks down the components of MBTI and gives example after example for understanding how personality influences our lives and how applying the power of understanding can be your most valuable tool in influencing and leading others both professionally and personally. Embrace and engage this knowledge and be the best you can be!

CHAPTER 1

POWER OF UNDERSTANDING

"Any fool can know. The point is to understand."
Albert Einstein

In my ten years as a counselor, I saw the transforming power of people coming to understand themselves and others better. That understanding turned broken relationships into loving, vibrant marriages. I will never forget one of my early counselees coming to that moment of understanding and acknowledging his powerlessness over drugs. He had been through a divorce, lost custody of his children, and was about to lose his job. However, as he gained an understanding of his addiction, he was able to start a process of recovery that helped him salvage his job, build a strong marriage, and then regain custody of his children.

In my ten years as a minister, I saw the power of young people developing a healthy understanding of who they were. It was exciting to see them use that understanding to make good choices over a wide range of important life decisions. The following is part of a recent note I received from a lady who was a young person in a church where I served about 42 years ago. The following describes how gaining an understanding of who she was as a teen led her to a very fulfilling career as a teacher: "I began to see something in myself as a quiet, shy teenager who had low self-esteem. I gained a confidence that I used to get a degree in elementary education where I retired after 33 years. I feel blessed."

Over the last 30 years, I have been associated with leaders who were dealing with a variety of organizational effectiveness issues. A major focus of my work has been helping to develop teams, employees, and leaders, and helping organizations to solve major problems and make the changes needed to improve organizational performance.

The first step in that development process was always gaining an understanding of the dynamics associated with the situation and the strengths and needs of the individual or group. Utilizing Stephen Covey's 4th habit of "seek first to understand, then to be understood" was always the starting point in addressing any need. As Covey emphasizes in this habit, we should never prescribe a solution before we diagnose the problem. By helping people develop a clear understanding of their problem or need, the answers to complex problems/needs were often easy to identify.

In observing successful individuals and leaders over these years, I found a key factor in their success was their desire and ability to develop an understanding of the situations they encountered and the problems they needed to solve. Their genius was less about being the smartest person in the room and more about recognizing the importance of diagnosing before prescribing.

One of the best examples of this was a situation involving my mother-in-law and a heart surgeon. My mother-in-law, Marjorie, was 82 years-old at the time and was facing open heart surgery for a triple by-pass. My wife, her sister, and I were in Marjorie's hospital room the night before her surgery and the surgeon who was scheduled to perform the surgery the next morning came into her room. We had not met him but had heard he was the best heart surgeon in town. He later moved to one of the leading heart centers in the country.

After introductions, the surgeon pulled up a chair and sat by Marjorie's bed. His first question was, "Marjorie, how are things going?" This seemed a little unusual to me considering the situation. This simple question started a 30-minute conversation about a variety of things. The surgeon really did not ask many additional questions. He listened and responded empathically to the things Marjorie shared. On a few occasions my wife or her sister would interject a comment and the surgeon would very politely look back at Marjorie and say, "Marjorie, how do you see that?" I thought to myself, "What is this surgeon doing?" He had the results from all the medical tests and understood exactly what was needed from a physical standpoint. Then it hit me. He was performing a difficult surgery the next morning on an 82-year-old woman. This surgery would involve a challenging and painful recovery. I realized that this "non-medical" discussion was really a "mental state" diagnosis of whether Marjorie was mentally and emotionally prepared for the surgery and a difficult recovery. After that 30-minute conversation, the surgeon looked at my mother-in-law with a smile and said, "I think we are ready, and I will see you in the morning Marjorie." He had completed his diagnosis and gathered the last piece of information he needed before performing this challenging surgery. His willingness to take the time to get to know and understand Marjorie also had a very calming effect on her.

We can see the power of understanding dramatically at the organizational or social level. Bill Gate's personal mission statement, which influenced the founding and incredible success of Microsoft, was "to see a computer on every desk and in every home." This mission becoming a reality demonstrates how understanding the potential of putting the computing power available to companies and governments into the hands of individuals has transformed our lives. Bill Gates is a genius, but the primary factor in this monumental accomplishment becoming a reality was his understanding of the implications of computing power for the individual and the technology that could transform a mainframe into a desktop computer.

Steve Jobs' genius was in understanding how technology could enable people to do things they had not even imagined with a small mobile electrical device that we can hold in our hands. Understanding what people need before they express it led Steve Jobs to build Apple and transform the way we live. So now my phone not only serves as my phone, but my computer, my GPS, my calendar, my camera, my mailbox, my banking tool, my TV, my phone book, my alarm clock, and so forth. It is hard to believe smart phones have only been around for thirteen years as I type this.

Every great invention or innovation begins with someone understanding a phenomenon, a problem, or a need in a unique way.

Even at a social level, understanding is critical to great advancements. Dr. Martin Luther King understood that the oppression Black people had experienced for centuries was also experienced by others in some ways. He also recognized this was not a black versus white issue. He recognized it was a human issue. Dr. King led a movement that fought for the civil rights of all people and engaged white people by appealing to a higher motive. History confirms our darker side promotes an "us versus them" world view. Dr. King understood no one really wins when we see the world that way. For Dr. King it was all about "us." He wanted everyone to rise together.

Understanding is powerful and is an ability that is essential if we are to be effective and successful in all areas of our lives. Acting before we understand will often lead to failure.

This book will advocate for a tool I have found to be immensely helpful in enabling people to understand themselves and others better. I will share many real-life stories of how I have seen this tool transform the lives of individuals, teams, and organizations over the last 48 years in my roles as a minister, counselor, professor, and organizational development consultant.

CHAPTER 2

HISTORY BEHIND THE MYERS-BRIGG TYPE INDICATOR (MBTI)

"Everything that irritates us about others can lead us to an understanding of ourselves."

Carl Jung

The tool we will explore for helping us develop a better understanding of ourselves and others is the Myers-Briggs Type Indicator or MBTI. The MBTI is the oldest and most used personality assessment instrument of its type in the world. MBTI was developed by the mother/daughter team of Katharine Briggs and Isabel Myers in 1942. Their objective was to apply certain theories about human behavior in a practical way to help integrate women into a traditionally male dominated workplace. During World War II, women went into the workplace due to the shortage of workers created by men being sent overseas to fight in the war. As a result of the work of Briggs and Myers, the MBTI helped to provide a framework for better understanding personality differences in the workplace.

The theories Isabel Myers and Katharine Briggs used to develop the framework on which MBTI is built were developed by Carl Jung.

Carl Jung's father was a pastor, and his grandfather was a physician. He was influenced in the field of psychology by Sigmund Freud and Alfred Adler and in the field of philosophy by Immanuel Kant and Friedrich Nietzsche. These great thought leaders informed Jung's practical psychology, and he drew from medicine, psychology, philosophy, religion, and anthropology to shape his views. However, integrating these views with what he observed in human behavior is the genius of his work. His psychology and certainly his concepts in relation to psychological types are very practical and applicable to our everyday life, and that is what this book will strive to demonstrate.

Carl Jung did not imagine his concepts being utilized to develop a personality assessment instrument. In fact, Jung expressed these thoughts about the inappropriateness of typing people: "Even in medical circles the opinion has got about that my method of treatment consists in fitting patients into this system and giving them corresponding "advice." My typology is far rather a critical apparatus serving to sort out and organize the welter of empirical material, but not in any sense to stick labels on people. It is not a physiognomy (way of judging character) and not an anthropological system, but a critical psychology dealing with the organization of delimiting of psychic processes that can be shown to be typical."

He added: "Although there are doubtless individuals whose type can be recognized this is by no means always the case. As a rule, only careful observation and weighing of the evidence permit a sure classification. However simple and clear the fundamental principle of the (opposing attitudes and functions) may be, in factual reality they are complicated and hard to make out, because every individual is an exception to the rule."

We will not dive deeply into the psychological theories of Jung nor the research on the MBTI as an assessment instrument. No personality assessment instrument is perfect, and MBTI is not. However, it is the most used and most researched instrument of its type. MBTI has been used for over 70 years in the following settings: for leadership development, personal effectiveness, teambuilding and other ways in business and industry; various usages in academic settings; career counseling; marriage and family counseling; and teambuilding in athletics and other settings. MBTI is used in 115 countries and in 88% of the Fortune 500 companies. Jung's typology and the MBTI, as an instrument, have withstood the test of time.

This book will give example after example of the value I have seen MBTI deliver in a variety of settings. However, I do want to cite a few factors that need to be considered in using the instrument and applying the concepts it measures.

1. The MBTI has comparable reliability (consistency of results when a person takes it again) to other instruments of its type. It also has comparable validity (measures what it says it measures). I am certified to use many personality instruments like MBTI, and they all are useful. None of them are perfect and all of them should not be treated like a dispensation from heaven about the true nature of an individual's personality. We are too complex and too many things, both nature and nurture, contribute to defining who we are. To expect an assessment instrument to utilize our response to a series of statements or questions to tell us who we are is absurd. What a good assessment instrument can do is provide a framework for better understanding the creatures we are. I have found MBTI to be extremely helpful for me and many others over the years.

2. MBTI is great for helping us to better understand ourselves and others, but it should never be used to put someone in a box that might limit the way we see them. Every person is different and even people with the same personality type will do things

very differently at times. This is one reason MBTI is not utilized for hiring or job placement of employees. People with diverse types can be equally successful in the same job. They will just approach things in diverse ways.

3. You are not just one preference or the other. MBTI measures our preference for one set of behaviors or the other on four dimensions of behavior. It is comparable to the preference we have for using our left or our right hand to write. Unless we are ambidextrous, we prefer using our right or our left hand. It does not mean we cannot use the other hand. It just means we have a preference for using one hand over the other. We can all get better at using our lesser preferences with practice. In fact, Jung said as we mature it gets harder and harder to identify an individual's preferences because we develop the ability to use our lesser preferred preferences more effectively with practice and when it is more beneficial in each situation.

Enough about the background of the MBTI, I am excited about sharing real stories of ways the knowledge and use of MBTI has helped people to better understand themselves and others in a way that enabled the transformation of people, teams, and organizations.

It is not necessary to know your MBTI Personality Type to benefit from reading this book. However, it might make it more interesting. For information about taking the MBTI, go to the following website: www.myersbriggs.org/my-mbti-personality-type/take-the-mbti-instrument.

CHAPTER 3

OVERVIEW OF MBTI

This book will examine the practical applications of MBTI and Jung's typology in personal and organizational settings I have observed over the last 48 years. I want to place special emphasis on the word practical. I have written one research dissertation and have no desire to ever write another one. There are also books written by authors who are much more knowledgeable than me on the concepts and theories related to MBTI. I am an MBTI practitioner. I have used MBTI with over 2,000 individuals and two hundred teams. This book will focus on stories of how I have seen individuals, teams and even organizations use MBTI to improve personal, interpersonal and team effectiveness. A student who had completed an MBA came up to me after one of my leadership courses and said: "Rick, you taught a lot of the same concepts I had in my MBA program, but the concepts really came alive in this course." As we talked more, he shared how the stories showing the concepts demonstrated in real life situations deepened his understanding of the concepts. I hope this book will do the same for you in relation to the MBTI. The book is less about describing MBTI and more about showing how the personal preferences MBTI measures plays out in real life.

As a psychologist, I will have to acknowledge a bias. My favorite person in the field of psychology is Carl Jung. Since his work was influenced by philosophy, psychology, medicine, religion, and years of observing people, he brings great breadth and depth to our understanding of psychology. Typology reflects a small part of his work and I have found all his concepts to be so informative in helping me understand basic human behavior. Typology is a theory of personality which helps us understand individuals by preference and type. He was truly a genius and as with geniuses, his thoughts at times are complex and not easy to understand.

This is where the work of Isabella Myers and Katharine Briggs becomes so important in relation to Jung's work on typology. They took Jung's insightful concepts related to typology and added two additional preferences which were implied in Jung's work. In addition, they developed the Myers-Briggs Type Indicator to measure an individual's four preferences and four-letter type. As discussed earlier, they applied Jung's concepts to address a real-world important problem. Integrating a large influx of women into the workforce had presented unanticipated challenges because women often approached work differently and organizations were looking for a way to understand those differences. This became the birthplace for MBTI and the popular application of Carl Jung's concepts related to typology. The MBTI has brought value to the workplace for over 75 years as indicated by its wide usage. Approximately 50% of the usage of MBTI today is in the workplace.

Jung identified three pairs of preferences. He called the first pair attitudes, and the two attitudes were *Extraversion* and *Introversion*. He observed that some people's orientation toward the world was directed more toward the external world of people and activities. These individuals with a preference for *Extraversion*, were energized by interactions with the external world. He also observed that other people were more focused on the internal world of reflection and contemplation. These individuals with a preference for *Introversion* were energized by going inside themselves to develop a deeper understanding of their world.

Before we examine the other preferences, I want to revisit a previous important concept which has to do with the clarity of a preference. The MBTI assessment is constructed such that there are questions related to each pair of preferences and the way you respond to each question will demonstrate a preference for one of the pair. For example, whether your response is more typical for an *Extravert* or more typical for an *Introvert*. If there are 20 *Extraversion/Introversion* questions and you responded like an *Extravert* on eighteen questions and like an Introvert on two, you would clearly be an *Extravert* and you would have a high score for *Extraversion*. On the other hand, if you answered eleven questions like an *Extravert* and nine like an *Introvert*, you would have an extremely low score on *Extraversion* and the clarity of your preference would not be strong.

There is nothing good or bad about having strong clarity on a preference. The degree of clarity will simply tell us something about our personality and behavior. Let me share an example. Zellie Earnest, the dear friend I mentioned in the acknowledgements had a score of 90+ on *Extraversion* and my score is below 10. Zellie seldom had introverted moments. He was constantly looking for interaction with the external world. In our work, we would travel overseas on occasions for weeks at a time. We would meet each other for breakfast and talk, talk, talk. We would then teach classes or lead workshops and have discussion after discussion. We would then go to dinner and talk some more. About 8 PM, I would look at Zellie and say: "Zellie, you are my best friend and I enjoy spending time with you as much as any person I know. However, I have had as much of you as I can take. I need a break. Can you please find someone else to talk to?" Zellie would just laugh and talk to a bellhop, a waiter, or any stranger that needed some interaction.

I was doing an MBTI workshop as a part of a leadership retreat years after my travel experiences with Zellie. Before the workshop, I shared with the group that if it were OK, I would leave my phone on because my sister had a serious illness, and I might be getting a call about her. They were very understanding, and later as I finished sharing the story about the strength of Zellie's *Extraversion* with the group, my phone rang. I excused myself, turned around and answered the phone. The voice on the other end replied, "Where are you?" It was Zellie. I turned to the class and said, "I'm sorry, it's Zellie and he needs some interaction." We all laughed at how the call supported in the story I was sharing.

Compared to Zellie, I look like an *Introvert*. If you put me with an *Introvert* who scores ninety on *Introversion*, I would look like a clear *Extravert*. There is disagreement about what the clarity of an individual's preference means but I have found over the years that people seem to fall in about three areas in relation to their clarity on any of the preferences. Depending on the range in which your score falls on each preference, you will have a high, moderate, or low clarity for that preference. For example, I have a low clarity of preference for *Extraversion* and that makes sense to me. The people who know me best would confirm I am an *Extravert* but also indicate I have some introverted characteristics. On the other hand, each of my other preferences, which are *Intuition*, *Feeling*, and *Perceiving*, are high in terms of clarity and those who know me well would tell you there is no doubt those are my preferences.

Understanding the concept of clarity of preference can also help us understand why we might get a different result when we take the assessment a second time. If the clarity of our preference is low, we are more likely to get a different preference on a subsequent assessment.

Extraversion/Introversion is the first pair of preferences. In looking at the next two pairs of preferences, Jung referred to them as functions. Jung observed that we are doing one of two things as we go through each day. We are either perceiving the world around us or judging the world which involves making decisions about things or organizing our world. In performing each of those two activities, we perform them in two distinct ways, thus our next two pair of preferences.

As we perceive the world, Jung found we did so either through *Sensing*, which involves using the five senses of hearing, seeing, touching, tasting, and smelling, or through *Intuition*, which utilizes a hunch or internal sense about what is going on around us. *Sensing* people are in tune with the real world in a very practical and realistic way. They live in the moment and notice smells, sounds, and visual images around them. *Intuitive* people on the other hand perceive the world through hunches about what is "really" happening or what will happen in the future. They live more in the future and less in the present or past. They see connections and patterns as opposed to specifics and details associated with the present situation. They see the forest not the trees.

Our next pair of preferences relate to what drives the judgments we make as we navigate the world around us. Jung found that some people used the preference of *Thinking* to make decisions. These people are very logical and rational in making decisions. They gather all the relevant facts and weigh the advantages and disadvantages, the pros and cons, and whichever way the scales tilt will determine the path they will choose. They would see this as the only logical thing to do. People with a preference for *Feeling*, on the other hand, approach decisions based on the impact of the decision upon people. For the *Feeling* person, decisions are much more subjective and focused on people and values versus on logic.

We have looked briefly at the three pairs of preferences which Carl Jung described. When Isabella Myers and Katharine Briggs began applying Jung's concepts of typology, they added a fourth pair of preferences. Jung described the four functions of *Sensing, Intuition, Thinking* and *Feeling* which deal with the ways we perceive and make judgments in relation to the world around us. Myers and Briggs built on this idea of Jung and concluded that people demonstrated a preference for the activities of *Judging* and *Perceiving*. They believed some people preferred

Judging and invested their energy more on making decisions, completing things, and keeping the world in order. They believed other people had a preference for *Perceiving* and focused their effort on observing and adapting to the world. People with a preference for *Perceiving* are curious and are more about starting things than finishing things.

In summary the four preferences address four basic questions that are critical to understanding human behavior.

1. Do I go inside or outside myself for energy?
2. Do I perceive the world around me with my five senses or through hunches and possibilities?
3. Do I make decisions based on logic and reason or the impact on people?
4. Do I organize and structure my life or observe and adapt to life?

Based on your preference in relation to those four questions, you will have four of the following preferences. I have included a brief description of the eight possible preferences and in bold you will see the letter assigned to each preference which we will use in describing the preferences throughout the book.

1. **E**xtraversion: People who get their energy from people and activities.
2. **I**ntroversion: People who get their energy from thought and reflection.
3. **S**ensing: People who observe the world through the five senses.
4. **IN**tuition: People who observe the world through hunches and possibilities.
5. **T**hinking: People who make decisions based on logic and reason.
6. **F**eeling: People who make decisions based on the impact on people.

7. Judging: People who seek to organize the world and complete things.

8. Perceiving: People who adapt to the world and start things.

The matrix below shows how our four preferences in relation to the four questions can be combined into sixteen different four-letter types. By understanding my four preferences and how they interact with each other and the preferences of others, I can enhance my self-understanding and understanding of others immensely. The chart is constructed in a manner that follows the following four patterns:

1. All the *Sensing* preferences are in the left two columns and the *Intuition* preferences are in the right two columns.

2. All the *Introversion* preferences are in the top two rows and the *Extraversion* preferences are in the bottom two roles.

3. All the *Feeling* preferences are in the middle two columns and the *Thinking* preferences are on outer two columns.

4. All the *Perceiving* preferences are in the middle two rows and the *Judging* preferences are in the top and bottom rows.

ISTJ	ISFJ	INFJ	INTJ
ISTP	ISFP	INFP	INTP
ESTP	ESFP	ENFP	ENTP
ESTJ	ESFJ	ENFJ	ENTJ

Myers and Briggs then built a personality assessment instrument around these four pairs of preferences, and it is what we know as the Myers-Briggs Type Indicator or MBTI. By taking the instrument, you can receive feedback on what your preferences are. By knowing my preference on each of the four pairs and seeing what my four-letter type is and the dynamics of how the preferences interact with one another, I can gain a helpful understanding of myself and others. I can gain insights about how the individual MBTI preferences influence my behavior and the results I get in my relationships, my work life and any area of my life that matters to me.

The rest of the book will share actual stories of how I have observed MBTI preferences and MBTI personality types influence the effectiveness of individuals, teams, and organizations. To assist in gaining the most from these stories, I would like to introduce a critical reflection process that can facilitate learning from these stories in a way which will help you better understand the underlying concepts in the stories. It will also help to apply those concepts in a way that will improve your effectiveness.

About 30 years ago, my dear friend, Zellie, taught me a straight-forward process for facilitating critical reflection and learning. The process involved asking the following three questions: What; So What; and Now What? Asking the *What* question helps us clarify the content about what we have read, heard, thought, felt, did, or observed. After identifying the *What*, it is important to ask the question *So What*. This encourages us to examine the meaning and implications of the things we have experienced. Finally, the *Now What* challenges us to move beyond the new insights and decide what we intend to do in relation to what we have learned.

At various points, I will share with you the *What, So What and Now What* from my viewpoint about the stories and concepts covered. I encourage you to identify the *What, So What and Now What* from what you have read.

Now we are ready to dive in.

- **What:** The Myers-Briggs Type Indicator (MBTI) is the most researched and utilized personality assessment instrument in the world. It is built upon a strong theory based on the work of Carl Jung and the practical development and application by Isabella Myers and Katharine Briggs. As with every other personality assessment, it is not perfect, but it is effective in helping us understand our behavior and the behavior of others.
- **So What:** The MBTI has helped millions of people to better understand themselves and others.
- **Now What:** We can utilize MBTI to harness the power of understanding ourselves and others to improve our ability to accomplish things, communications, personal relationships, decision-making, teamwork, organizational effectiveness, and functioning in our world each day.

CHAPTER 4

INFLUENCE OF THE EXTRAVERSION/INTROVERSION (E/I) PREFERENCE

I saw the power of the *E/I* preference daily as a father to my daughter and son. Kelly, my daughter, was the first born and it was obvious by the time she was two that she was an *Introvert*. It was evident because she loved us reading to her and grew to love reading herself. I can recall, even before she was two, reading book after book to her and then re-reading the books. We read the books so many times that I would deliberately pause at times and Kelly would finish the sentence.

Kelly's *Introversion* has continued to this day. As a 49-year-old, she is a college professor and is still energized by going inside herself. She continues to love reading and developing a deep understanding of her areas of interest. She has close relationships and is very capable in teaching and social settings, but quiet, intimate times are her cup of tea.

My son, Chris, came along two years after Kelly and his preference was clearly for *Extraversion*. He would watch me read to Kelly and wanted to get in on the action. He would hop up into my lap with a book, and I would begin to read. After about ten pages, he would jump down and do something else. He never became a big reader. Rather than going inside for energy, Chris found his energy in interactions with people and activities in the external world.

Chris is forty-seven now and over the years he has continued to demonstrate his preference for *Extraversion*. He has multiple networks of friends like his high school friends, his college friends, his Charlotte friends, his Rio de Janeiro friends, his tennis friends, his volleyball friends, and others. While driving to see a Tennessee football game years ago, he said, "Dad did I tell you that I'm going to see Tennessee play Alabama in Tuscaloosa?" I said no, and then asked him how he was going to be able to do that. He said, "Well I have a friend who has some tickets, and we're going down and stay with another friend's grandmother." A year or so later, we were going to get something to eat, and he said, "Hey dad did I tell you I'm going to Chicago during the NBA finals and I'm hoping to see Michael Jordan and the Bulls play?" I asked how he was going to be able to pull that off. He said, "Well my college roommate is trying out for a professional European team, and he is going to Chicago for the tryout, so I am going to with him. I asked him how you are going to get there. Chris replied, "Well I have a friend who is a pilot with an airline, and he is giving me a pass." I then asked how they were going to get tickets for the game. Chris indicated they had not figured that out yet. As it turned out, they went to Chicago and on the day of the game they got to know a vendor who let them work selling shirts all day in exchange for two tickets. Five minutes before tipoff Chris and his roommate were in their seats to see Michael Jordan and the Bulls in an NBA finals game.

Chris has served in Mother Teresa's ministries in India because of the relationships he builds. He has also chosen careers like coaching, teaching and being a minister that fit his *Extraversion* very well. You could see his *Extraversion* when he was two, and it is still obvious today.

E/I Impact on Interpersonal Relationships

Introverts are energized by going inside themselves. They love to focus on one thing at a time and consider it deeply without distractions, and they end up knowing a lot about a few things. They do not naturally express what they are thinking, so if you want to know what an Introvert thinks, you will need to ask. The *Extravert*, on the other hand, is energized by external interactions with people and activities. They enjoy moving from one thing to another and knowing a little about a lot of things. They love to be involved in lots of things at the same time. The expression "think out loud" describes them well, because instead of thinking and then speaking like the *Introvert*, they think as they speak so they often stick their feet in their mouths. If you want to know what an *Extravert* thinks, all you need to do is listen. They will tell you.

Extraverts can overwhelm *Introverts* with lengthy interactions, and *Introverts* can frustrate *Extraverts* by not making them aware of valuable information. I want to share a few personal and professional examples that will illustrate the potential problems in the relationship between *Extraverts* and *Introverts* and things that can be done intentionally to minimize the problems and maximize the synergy between these two preferences.

In a counseling situation with a couple concerning a challenge they were having in their marriage it became obvious that their issue had a lot to do with her being a clear *Introvert* and him being a clear *Extravert*. I asked them to take the MBTI, and it confirmed what I thought about their *E/I* preferences.

What enabled me to correctly identify their preferences and the issue in their marriage was how they described the problems they were experiencing. The wife was a customer service representative in an insurance agency, and the husband was a teacher who dealt with wild and crazy kids all day. When they would get home after an exhausting day of work and many interactions with customers and students, they had to decide how to spend that critical time in the afternoon and evening as a young couple.

For the introverted wife, she was drained of energy from nine continuous hours of interacting with customers on issues related to their insurance. She came home with a need for quiet time alone to reflect, contemplate, and go inside. As a result, she would go into the den and get immersed in reading, and any interaction with the husband she loved dearly was avoided because of that need for quiet time. The husband interpreted this lack of interest in conversation or doing something together right after work as a personal rejection, and it hurt. He could not understand why the people he worked with and the children he taught loved to interact with him while his wife did not.

For the extraverted husband, he wanted to come home and do something with his wife or with her and friends. His interactions at work energized him and created a desire for more external stimulation. As a result, when he came home and would push for doing things together or with others, his wife thought he was invading her space and was not understanding of her needs. She felt like he was being pushy and inconsiderate.

After they received their MBTI results, we discussed how their natural behavioral preferences were driving their behavior and not insensitivity to each other's needs. Part of what had attracted him to her was her quiet, thoughtful, and calming influence. Part of what attracted her to him was his outgoing, energetic spirit that was always open to doing new things. Understanding both the strengths and pitfalls of *Extraversion* and *Introversion* helped them examine their behavior constructively. They laughed at the way these differences influenced their relationship in interesting and often amusing ways. They were able to see these differences as natural behavior demonstrated throughout their lives, as opposed to something they were doing to each other with a lack of consideration for one another.

This simple understanding of one another's behavior was the most crucial factor in making the problems they were experiencing very manageable. That mutual understanding also led to some changes in behavior that helped to move their relationship in a positive direction. That challenging time each day after work became different. They decided that each day after work, before they would begin their shared time together, she would come home and have an hour to read by herself, and he would go next door and bother the neighbors. May have been a slight problem for the neighbors at times, but it worked great for the couple.

E/I Impact on Working Relationships

Over the years I have used MBTI preferences in the workplace, there are countless times it has helped me to understand challenges in certain relationships and find ways to overcome those challenges.

I spent 28 years of my life working for a large multi-national Fortune 500 company (which I will refer to as Company A throughout the book). For the last part of my career my role was in organizational development. In that role, I was like an internal consultant and did executive coaching, leadership development, organizational design, change management, team building, and group facilitation.

I often worked with the senior leadership on a variety of issues. There was one member of the Executive Team who I worked with on occasion, and we just never clicked. It was a struggle to develop a productive working relationship. I was teaching an MBTI class one day and was pointing out how *Extraverts* talk and then think, and *Introverts* think and then talk and how this can create communication problems. As we were discussing this difference, I realized this was the source of the problem I was having with the senior executive. He was a strong *Introvert*, and I am an *Extravert*. I thought back on several ineffective interactions and they would typically start with this executive asking me a question about an organizational issue. As an *Extravert*, I would begin throwing ideas out as I "thought out-loud." As this stream of consciousness came out, it was a little disjointed and not well thought out.

After a few minutes, the senior executive would look at his watch and say "Rick, I'm sorry but I have an appointment and I'll get back to you." He did not get back with me because what he had heard from me made no sense to him. As a clear *Introvert*, he would never consider sharing something with someone unless he had thoroughly thought it through. His disjointed thinking would take place inside his head, and you would never hear a thought from him until it was clear and concise.

In our interactions, he would hear those jumbled initial thoughts from me that would have taken place inside his head. If he had listened to me another five minutes, I would have arrived at an idea that he might have found to be of value and helpful. This recognition of what was happening in our interactions was like a huge light going on and gave me hope I could improve that relationship.

Months later, the company was preparing for a major change. Very few people in the organization were aware of it, but I had become involved in the planning effort. I happened to be walking down the hallway of our executive offices, and this senior manager invited me to step into his office. He asked me if I was aware of the upcoming changes, and I indicated I was. He then asked me what the best practices were in managing this type of organizational change. My impulse as an *Extravert* was to start talking, but I knew this executive did not want a conversation but a very concise answer. I responded with, "Could I give that some thought and get back to you tomorrow?" A huge smile came across his face, and his thought was probably, "I am so happy I don't have to listen to Rick ramble on and on." I went back to my office, researched the challenges this change would face and talked to a trusted colleague. The next day, I sent the executive an email because I knew, as an *Introvert*, he would prefer an email over a phone call. In the email, I outlined the best practices for managing this type of change and what I would recommend we do. Within ten minutes, he sent me an email response and said my suggestion looked great and asked me to get with the project manager for the change effort and put those recommendations into action. The actions we took because of those recommendations were important in helping that change be successful. If I had interacted with the senior executive without understanding his preferred way of communicating, we would not have managed that change as successfully.

E/I Impact on Teamwork

MBTI in general and the preferences are powerful tools to use in teambuilding and team development. The *E/I* preference has a significant impact because it influences the way we communicate, and effective communication is critical to team success.

One thing I discovered over the years is at times teams are very predictable in terms of what they will look like on *E/I*. For example, in Company A, we had a large sales force and about 75% of our sales employees were *Extraverts*. Research supports the fact that more *Extraverts* gravitate toward sales related jobs due to the nature of the work and the fact that interactions with the external world is normally required. One thing we observed in working with sales management was that the *E/I* preference was not a predictor of effectiveness in the sales role. In other words, introverted sales representatives were just as effective as the extraverted sales representatives. They tended to approach the job a little differently, but they were still effective in the external interactions required.

We had two work groups in Company A that were about 90% introverted. *Introversion* was a dominant preference in both accounting and our research organizations, and this is not surprising when you consider the nature of their work. Accountants are working with data all day and making sure those numbers "add up." The scientists in our research organization were working all day in labs trying to understand the properties, make-up, and reactions of those molecules. Both of those roles were looking into things deeply for understanding.

We were going through a major organizational change, and it was going to have a tremendous impact on our accounting departments. I was working with them on responding to the transitions associated with those changes in a healthy and constructive manner. In doing that, I conducted a three-hour workshop for all the employees in accounting. These workshops had about forty employees in each workshop and were designed to be very interactive (I am an *Extravert*) with numerous small group discussions. I scheduled the workshops over several days with a morning and afternoon session. During and after the first workshop, I was really struggling. I felt like I was pulling teeth. It seemed to me there was little interaction, and I thought "this is not working." I had asked them to complete an evaluation of the workshop and with great anticipation I began reading the evaluations in hopes of finding something that might help me improve the afternoon session. To my surprise, they rated the workshop as excellent and included comments like these: loved the interactions; really enjoyed the opportunity to discuss the upcoming change; and great discussions. My initial reaction was shock, and then it hit me. Most of the participants were *Introverts*, and they were interacting at a level that was good for them. That afternoon I relaxed and did not push for *Extraversion* level participation. I changed a couple of the activities to be more one on one interactions and less large group discussion, which I knew would be a better fit for this group.

When working with teams, we explore how communication plays out on their team, and we look at the number of *Extraverts* and *Introverts* who are on their team. We then determine what might be influencing the communications within the team. From this, we begin to identify things each member of the team can do with some intentionality to help improve communications and team effectiveness. Some of the type of things that might come out of that analysis would be for the team to be more intentional about seeking the rich, thoughtful, and deep input from the *Introverts* on the team. It could also include *Extraverts* recognizing the need to leverage their ability to stimulate interaction while not dominating discussions and being more concise in their communications.

A senior management leader I worked with was a strong and clear *Extravert*. He was also brilliant and without intending could intimidate people with his level of knowledge on most aspects of the company's business. He came to realize that his natural tendency to think aloud and be energized by sharing his thoughts externally could be perceived as a "know it all" attitude. This was not an accurate reflection of his real mindset. As a result, when he was leading his team or any group, he was very intentional about posing issues and never expressing his viewpoint until everyone had expressed their perspective. If someone did not express a viewpoint, he would say something like, "John, you have not shared what you think about this issue, and I would really like to have your input." After everyone had expressed their thoughts on the topic, the senior leader would then express his thoughts. He utilized this approach with his team when they were making decisions. If the discussion was moving toward agreement on a path which was close to where he thought they needed to go, he never expressed a position on the decision because he wanted them to recognize the importance and power of their participation.

E/I Impact on Organizations

The individual preference percentage can tell you a lot about the personality and behavior of an organization. I would like to use my experience with one organization to show how MBTI can be used in a powerful way to help the organization understand itself and use MBTI to improve the way they work together and serve their members or customers.

Over the last sixteen years, I have been fortunate to work extensively with an organization (will refer to this organization as Company B throughout the rest of the book), which is a regional financial institution. It has approximately 1,000 employees and serves over 250,000 members. In its peer group of 5,000 plus organizations, it ranks in the top forty-three on all ten criteria used to measure organizational performance and in the top twenty on five of those criteria. Company B is recognized as one of the top performers in its area of business.

I do the leadership training for this organization which involves two four-day courses that all leaders go through within the first two years of being in their leadership role. I also teach a case study course in organizational performance and strategic planning that many of the more experienced leaders go through. In addition to those courses for leaders, I have taught a two-day personal effectiveness course and a half day MBTI course that all employees take. I also do some teambuilding and organizational development work as needed.

In addition to the half-day MBTI course that all employees attend, the two leadership courses utilize MBTI as a part of the coaching and team development sections of the leadership training. As a result, MBTI is a part of the organizational vocabulary and culture.

In each course, we examine examples of how MBTI is used to help this organization grow and improve.

In relation to the *E/I* preference, Company B has demonstrated how there has been an interplay between the mission, vision and values of this organization and the *Extraversion* and *Introversion* preferences. The major focus of this organization is to serve its members and be their preferred financial institution. Their motto is in effect, "We are beside you." There is a strong emphasis on having effective relationships with members and each other. This active interaction with others certainly sounds like an organization with a strong preference for *Extraversion*. This organization does not use MBTI for selection. As I have mentioned, MBTI is not valid for that use. However, they do use a very sound targeted selection process that looks for people who are effective in interacting with others.

As a result of this strong relational focus, it is not surprising that about 60% of the employees are *Extraverts*. In the operations areas, which includes the branches where tellers and member service representatives interact with members every day, over two thirds of the employees are *Extraverts*. Normally, about half the population are *Extraverts* and half are *Introverts*. This demonstrates that *Extraverts* have a stronger preference for member facing roles. It is also not surprising that the back-office roles like accounting and IT have a higher percentage of *Introverts*.

This organization has done an excellent job of using an understanding of how various parts of the organization is energized to improve cross functional relationships. For example, the introverted leader of the IT organization is very explicit about the natural tendency that IT might have for not communicating in person to the extent needed. As a result, the IT organization seeks to communicate more openly and solicits feedback to determine if more communication is needed.

- **What:** Differences in *Extraversion* and *Introversion* can create misunderstandings and conflicts in relationships.
- **So What:** By understanding another person's natural and preferred way of interacting with others, I can better accept their way of interacting and not interpret their responses in a way that hurts the relationship.
- **Now What:** I will seek to create a common ground where others are able to express their thoughts, feelings, and views in their preferred way of interacting while also enabling me to express mine.

CHAPTER 5

INFLUENCE OF THE SENSING/INTUITION (S/N) PREFERENCE

A s previously mentioned, the *S/N* preference deals with how we perceive the world. Jung observed that some people, who he described as *Sensing*, perceived the world through the five senses of seeing, hearing, touching, tasting, and smelling. They are very in tune with the immediate things in their environment that stimulate the senses. Other people who Jung said used *Intuition* observe or perceive the world through hunches about the possibilities around them and how things are related to or connected with something.

One way I can describe the differences in the way persons with *Sensing* and *Intuition* perceive the world around them is to imagine two people with these preferences being in a large classroom for a couple of hours for the first time. After coming out of the room, if you asked them to describe the room, they would describe the room in quite diverse ways. If you ask the *Sensing* person what the room is like, he/she would give you accurate details about: the shape of the room; the color of the walls and the floors; the furniture that was in the room and

29

the layout of the room; and whether it had projectors, white-boards, or other learning tools. If you then asked the person with a preference for *Intuition*, they would say something like, "Well I don't remember a lot about it, but if you cleared everything out of that room, it would be a wonderful place to play ping pong." Or they might say, "I don't remember a lot about it, but it is a lot like the room we were in for the workshop last week." If you will notice, the *Intuition* person did not perceive what the room was but what it could be used for or what it was like. People with a preference for *Intuition* perceive the following: what could be instead of what is; what it is like instead of what it is; and implications for the future and not what has been.

If you begin thinking about why this preference is so important in relation to understanding, just consider the importance of what we notice every day and how what we notice influences where we focus our energy. The *Sensing* person is gathering information in a very practical and realistic way and so they are influenced primarily by the realities of the world. They utilize the realities they have observed as inputs into decisions and actions. The *Intuitive* person on the other hand tends to overlook the practical realities of life and relentlessly pursues a new and different path unrestrained by practical realities. Those with a preference for *Intuition* are looking back at the *Sensing* person saying, "Come on, I know it's never been done but let's try anyway." The *Sensing* person is looking at the *Intuitive* saying: "You are living in the clouds, don't you know a bunch of people have tried that and failed."

The way we perceive the world has a tremendous impact on our ability to understand others. If I am unaware that people perceive the world differently and that each has merit, I will overlook information about some aspect of the past, present, or future. If I am a *Sensing* person, I need to recognize the world is full of things we became aware of for the first time and were the hunches of someone who perceived that possibility. As a person with a preference for *Intuition*, I need to recognize that at times I do overlook or fail to recognize practical limitations that are important to consider in relation to hunches and possibilities I may envision.

Valuing differences is a major benefit associated with understanding the preferences and types associated with MBTI. Over the years, I have certainly observed that in relation to this preference, and we will look at a few examples of this.

S/N Impact on Interpersonal Relationships

To explore the influence of the S/N preference on interpersonal relationships, I will take a huge risk and share about my relationship with my wife, Marcie. I will let you know that Marcie is the sweetest and kindest person I have ever known, and I do not believe I am biased. However, our difference on the S/N preference has been the greatest challenge for us in our relationship.

Marcie has a clear preference for *Sensing*, and I have a clear preference for *Intuition*. Marcie lives in the moment and is very in tune with everything that is going on around her. I am not always in touch with the practical details of the events around us, but I will have strong hunches about what those events mean and what implications they have for the future. Marcie loves to take her time and enjoy the experience, and I am always looking to the next thing and wanting to try something new.

A funny way this difference plays out with us is related to physical changes in our house. Marcie notices anything that changes immediately. She sees it, smells it, or hears it. I will never notice those physical changes. If Marcie gets something new like a lamp, a painting, or tablecloth, I usually will not notice it for weeks unless she tells me about it. Shortly before her father died, he started greeting everyone with the phrase, "shore do love you." This became something we would all say in greeting one another. Marcie found a little wood carving with those words, and she bought it and put it on our mantle over our fireplace.

One evening weeks later, I was sitting on the couch and Marcie came over, sat down, and put her head on my shoulder. As she put her head on my shoulder, I looked up at the mantle and saw the carving for the first time and thought, "that's new." After a moment, Marcie asked if I had noticed anything new in the living room, and I responded with, "sure, the carving on the mantle." She took her head off my shoulder and looked at me in surprise and said, "when did you notice it?" I responded, "about 10 seconds ago."

Not perceiving new hairdos and other things that are important to Marcie gets me in trouble at times, but Marcie has grown to understand that not noticing things around me is part of who I am. The biggest problem we have with our *S/N* difference is in planning vacations and other activities. Marcie as a *Sensing* person is very practical and as an *Intuitive* person, I am all about possibilities. When we are planning our day or a vacation, I can produce all kinds of things we could do. When I start spouting those things out, Marcie's first response is often: "Honey, I don't think we have time to do all of those things." And many times, all right most of the time, she is right. However, often we do get everything done or at least more than seemed possible.

A fitting example of this struggle is a trip we made several years ago. We live about 90 minutes from Knoxville, TN, and we were going there with plans to see an early movie at our favorite arts theatre and then have dinner and see a Tennessee basketball game that night. Prior to our marriage, Marcie would not have tackled that in one day, but we had pulled it off before, so she was ready to go. A few days before our day trip, I noticed a car dealership in Knoxville was having a sale and they had an SUV in which we were interested. I asked Marcie if we could leave a couple of hours earlier than planned and go by and check out the SUV. She said, "you aren't thinking about trying to trade today." Here is where I might have been a little less than forthright. I said, "probably not but could we just go by and see what they have to offer." She said, "well OK as long as we don't trade and miss the movie or anything we had planned." I thought that was great and so we added a couple of hours to our trip to go by that dealership.

Well to make a long story short, we found and traded for the exact SUV we wanted, got a great deal, and while they prepped the SUV, we got a loaner to go eat and see the movie so we could pick up the new SUV on our way to the game. Now, in all honesty, I can tell you there have been many occasions when Marcie was right, and we were not able to fit that one more activity into our plans. As my mother told me before we were married, "I am so happy you are marrying Marcie. She will slow you down." My mother was so right, and I have benefited in so many ways.

However, what we have discovered over the last twenty-two years is that Marcie helps me be more realistic in the things I try to do, and I help Marcie stretch and do things she did not think were possible. We usually have a practical plan with a couple of "stretch goals' that we pursue when possible. The understanding of and managing our S/N difference has been a major benefit in our relationship.

S/N Impact on Working Relationships

Being on the same page is an expression we use a lot in the workplace to emphasize the importance of being focused on the same issue and having a mutual understanding of what we have decided and plan to do. Since the S/N preference addresses how we perceive the world around us, it can have a significant impact on where people focus their energy. For example, the *Sensing* person is focused on details. They want every "t" crossed and every "i" dotted. The person with a preference for *Intuition*, on the other hand, does not pay attention to details. They focus their attention on the big picture and how different things are connected. This difference in focus can create a lot of wasted effort, poor decisions and actions that move us in different directions. It is critical to work from a mutual understanding of issues we are addressing and the relevant information in relation to those issues.

I recall observing a manager and an employee navigate this difference very well due to their collective understanding of each other's preferences. They understood how to avoid problems that are associated with having a different perception of issues. By using the strengths associated with each of their preferences, they created a synergy which improved the results on the projects they completed together. The manager was a self-proclaimed micro-manger and tended to focus not only on key details but every detail. The employee was a creative designer who was great at producing novel solutions to problems. If the designer got too far down in the details, it limited his creativity and problem-solving.

As they developed their manager/employee relationship, they used a mutual understanding of MBTI to talk about the strengths and challenges of their working relationship. Some of their similarities on preferences meant they each needed to make sure they did not miss something. For example, they both had a preference for *Thinking*, which meant they might have a tendency to overlook the people impact on issues. This resulted in them being very intentional about asking the following question: What effect do these actions have on anyone impacted by this project?

They realized their difference on the S/N preference would enable them to utilize each other's preference to ensure they were less likely to overlook details or new possibilities. However, this could be a source of conflict. The manager could get down in the weeds in a way that would distract the employee from using his strength of finding new and better ways to resolve problems. As a result, during the planning process for a project, they would identify the critical details that the manager needed. The employee then knew the critical details that he needed to manage and did not have to be bound by excessive focus on things that would limit his innovation.

S/N Impact on Teamwork

Oftentimes MBTI is useful in getting people's attention about how their preferences are affecting their choices and behavior. At times it takes something else to highlight how their preferences might be creating problems they do not see. That was the case with a Human Resources leadership team I worked with some years ago. I had done MBTI with them, and they were familiar with their individual and team preferences. Most of the team members were *Sensing* which contributed at times to an excessive attention to details. This attention to details was reinforced by a culture of perfectionism in relation to details and having the role of the preserver of the rules and guidelines for the organization. At times this was a source of frustration for employees in HR and the people for whom they provided support in the rest of the organization.

As a part of an officers' retreat, my colleague, Zellie, and I had utilized an instrument called the Organizational Culture Inventory (OCI) to help assess the culture of the Officers' Team and the rest of the organization. We did random samplings of various businesses and functions of the organization. With this instrument, you would examine the current and ideal culture of an organization and then identify cultural gaps which might adversely impact desired results. We would then work with the leaders of organizations to identify interventions to eliminate those cultural gaps and create a more constructive culture.

The HR leadership team wanted to do a cultural assessment of their team. They completed the assessments, and I had gotten their results and was scheduled to share them with the team. I came in a few minutes before I was scheduled to present the results of the OCI. There was someone presenting before me, and the discussion went much longer than they expected so we only had about fifteen minutes to share and discuss their results. Their three dominant cultural styles were: conventional, which meant they like to do things in a standard and repetitive manner; perfectionistic which meant they want everything to be done without error; and, oppositional which meant at times they would disagree for the sake of disagreeing without obvious reasons.

After I presented the results, they began picking the instrument apart asking questions about the way the data was normalized. I had never had a group raise those questions. They said they did not agree with the cultural styles from their assessment even though they had completed the assessments and it was just feeding them back what they had said in their responses. As they challenged their results, the noon hour struck and some of them had luncheon appointments. The VP of HR said "Rick, sorry that we have not had time to really consider these results. Would you come back next week, and we will complete our discussion?"

I was in the Training department at that time and my manager was a member of the HR management team. He saw me later in the day and asked me how I thought the OCI discussion had gone. I told him that it had gone exactly how I thought it would. With a puzzled look, he asked me what I meant. I said "You all responded in the way you do with all employees who present to the HR leadership team. Secondly, the OCI, which you all completed by answering questions about the way you work together, indicated you all are perfectionistic and oppositional. The team proceeded to act consistent with that assessment by picking the results apart and disagreeing with the assessment which simply reflected your team's responses to the questions." I was fortunate to have a manager who could handle and in fact appreciated direct feedback. His jaw dropped and he laughed and said, "oh my gosh, we did."

In the next presentation to the HR leadership team, my manager shared with the rest of the team our interaction. We continued the review of the results and had a very productive discussion. A major part of that discussion was talking about how the dominance of *Sensing* on their team was a major contributor to their excessive attention to details and expecting a level of perfection which was not always needed.

It began a journey for this team which resulted in them applying a form of the Pareto Principle. The Pareto Principle, or the law of the vital few, says that, for many events, 80% of the effects come from 20% of the causes. The team became much better at realizing that often-times investing 20% of our time in getting an 80% solution was much better than investing five times as much time to only gain an additional 20% of benefit. They began focusing more on the vital details and not the lesser important ones.

To illustrate the issues teams who have a dominance of *Intuition* might encounter, I would like to share about work I did with a marketing team. I have had the opportunity to work with several marketing groups over the years and most of them were dominant in *Intuition*. When you consider the nature of their work, being dominant in *Intuition* makes sense. They are looking for new and creative ways to market a product of service. This group was experiencing significant conflict about different ideas for promoting their products. Since *Intuitive* people perceive the world through hunches, their ideas are often not based on data or concrete events. Instead, they have this sixth sense that something is going to happen or will work. People with a preference for *Intuition* have been doing this their entire lives, and they become good at it. As a person with strong *Intuition*, my hunches are right most of the time, but not always. Sometimes, realities that we did not observe or were not aware of will come up behind us and give us a swift kick. However, until it happens, we are deeply convinced our *Intuition* is right and we will defend our perception until the end.

This marketing team was having some major conflicts. It was becoming personal and creating tension within the team. We looked at the dominance of *Intuition* on the team and how it was contributing to the conflict, because even though several were alike in their preference for *Intuition*, their intuitions were often not the same, and they all believed their hunches were right. Down deep, they all knew they were not always right, but in the heat of the moment this was at times forgotten.

With these insights about *Intuition*, the team committed to brainstorming potential ideas and not becoming entrenched in defending their idea. After they had completed the brainstorming process, they would consider the merits of each idea and looked to the *Sensing* members of the team to help bring in practical considerations that the Ns might have overlooked. They discovered that frequently the *Sensing* team members would bring out things that would make one of the ideas generated by an N obviously impossible. And oftentimes, the *Intuition* person who generated the idea would be the first to recognize it. This process made the interactions within this team much more productive and pleasant.

S/N Impact on Organizations

Company B has an employee population that looks a lot like the general population for the *S/N* preference. About 75% of the general population is *Sensing* and about 25% is *Intuition*. I have told people over the years that once you understand MBTI, so many things make sense. It is good that 75% of the population is *Sensing*, because if only 25% were *Sensing* nothing would ever work. We need some people who see the big picture and focus on the future and not the details at hand. However, running day to day activities that need practical and accurate attention is important to our world functioning day in and day out. This is the reason we need more people with a preference for *Sensing*.

Company B's financial organization is about two-thirds *Sensing* and one-third *Intuition*, which is a little unusual for a financial institution. Financial institutions tend to be even more *Sensing* dominant because they are dealing with numbers and making sure those numbers have a high degree of accuracy. Certainly, this financial institution has enough *Sensing* to ensure the needed attention is given to details. However, the prominent level of *Intuition* is evident in their use of scenario planning to prepare for unanticipated future events. They did not fall into the "bean counter" trap that some financial organizations fall into.

In addition, this organization is seen as a very innovative and visionary financial institution. A lot of this forward thinking has been driven by a senior leadership team which has strong *Intuition*. Their CEO over a 21-year period that recently ended was an ENTJ and a clear preference for *Intuition*. Many visionary leaders are ENTJs, and this leader would fall into that category.

Having worked with this leader at various points in his career, I have seen very few leaders who truly grasped the concepts of MBTI and how to apply them like this leader did. He was great at understanding how MBTI was influencing other people and how to use that awareness to create a better relationship with them.

A significant way in which he used an understanding of his clear *Intuition* was ensuring his *Intuition* did not become a problem for the organization. His *Intuition* was invaluable in the ways he used it to forge strategic initiatives that sparked significant growth. When I first worked with him in 1999, shortly after he became CEO, the organization had fewer than one hundred employees and only two stand-alone branches in the area. Today the organization has about 1,000 employees and twenty-six branches in their home geographic area.

Frequently, leaders who are visionary can get too far out in front of practical realities and limitations in pursuing strategic initiatives. While leading this organization in an aggressive and innovative way, he was always able to balance his future oriented *Intuition* with the practical considerations impacting employees and the capacity of the organization in the present. In other words, he understood the importance of the *Sensing* perspective and learned to develop the capability to use it.

On several occasions over the years, I would go to him with ideas about an organizational development initiative which I was convinced would be of excellent value to the organization. We would have an enthusiastic conversation and he would often share how he thought my proposal was a great idea. And then, he would look at me and say something like this: "Rick, as much value as I see to what you are proposing, our employees already have a lot on their plate in pursuit of our two strategic goals for the year, and I do not want to add something else that might distract them from those goals or place undue stress on them." What a rejection! I never felt hurt or disappointed when he rejected my idea, because I knew he was right. As an MBTI practitioner, I always came away impressed with how this person with clear *Intuition* understood how to use his lesser preferred *Sensing* function to keep the organization focused on the vital few and only stretch the organization when it was mission critical.

- **What:** Differences in *Sensing* and *Intuition* has a tremendous influence on the way we perceive the world around us and can create significant misunderstandings based on those diverse perspectives.
- **So What:** By understanding the differences in the way we perceive the same situation, we can be open to seeing things we might naturally miss, and this will help us understand the other person's viewpoint.
- **Now What:** By combining the perspective our preference naturally perceives with the perspective of the opposite preference, we will have a more complete view of situations and create new possibilities instead of conflict in relationships.

INFLUENCE OF THE THINKING/FEELING (T/F) PREFERENCE

The *Thinking/Feeling (T/F)* preference is the decision-making function of MBTI. It deals with how we approach decisions and the primary factors we initially consider in making decisions. The person with a preference for *Thinking* approaches decisions from a very logical perspective. People with a preference for *Thinking* gather all the facts and evidence, and then weigh the evidence like the Scales of Justice which symbolizes our legal system. Whichever way the scales tilt, they choose that path. They would not consider choosing the side that was outweighed because that would not be logical.

On the other hand, people with a preference for *Feeling* approach decisions based on how the decision impacts people. They consider the implication of the decision for those who will be affected and attempt to make the decision which has the most positive effect on the people involved or at least the ones that matter most. They want to maximize the positive impact for those affected, and they try their best to do no harm to anyone. Logic is secondary to a consideration of personal impact.

People who have a preference for *Feeling* have no problem setting aside logic and fairness for unique treatment of people. Those who are *Feeling* have no problem with a decision varying from situation to situation. Being consistent in situations is not as important for an *F*.

The most interesting place for me to study this preference has been in the workplace. As a minister, counselor, and teacher, being a clear *F* was very natural and accepted. On the other hand, in my 28 years of working for a chemical company, being an *F* was often a challenge. Most of the professional employees I worked with were engineers, accountants, IT staff, and management. Those career choices are heavily dominated by *T*s. When I say heavily, I am talking about 80% plus. As we were considering and making business decisions, most of the people I worked with were looking at the decision from one perspective and I was looking at it from another. This could have been very frustrating and problematic at times, but by understanding *T/F* dynamic, I was able to turn it into an opportunity and a strength. I was able to bring a different and important perspective to the table in many situations.

This was Company A, and although we did not use MBTI as extensively as we do in Company B, most of the people I worked with understood MBTI. As a result, we could use the concepts of MBTI to help us understand the differences in the way we were looking at decisions and the merits of each of those viewpoints. I was able to demonstrate to them I saw the value of the logic used to make decisions, and I knew they cared about people so I could bring issues related to the impact on people into the discussion. They would often see the importance of those people implications and would throw that piece of "evidence" into the analysis of the decision.

One of the best illustrations of how this balancing of *Thinking* and *Feeling* can be accomplished was in the employee disciplinary review process. In my role as an Employee Assistance Counselor, an employee would often ask me to sit in on a disciplinary review meeting as an advocate for them. On one occasion, a gentleman who had come to work under the influence of alcohol asked me to attend his disciplinary review meeting. Other people in the meeting were the employee's management and representatives of Human Resources. Most of them were engineers, managers, and men. About two-thirds of men are *Ts* and two-thirds of women are *Fs*, which is the only gender difference of the MBTI preferences. Most of the men were *Ts* and came from work groups that are dominated by *T*. I knew we were in for a very logical discussion, and it was exactly that. A major part of the discussion went something like this: "Six months ago, John came to work under the influence, and we gave him a month off without pay, placed him on final warning, and required him to get assistance through the Employee Assistance Program. Since we did that with John, we should do the same with Bill." It was hard to argue with that logic and the decision would certainly be fair, consistent, and easy to justify.

But then an *F* spoke up and said: "I know what we did with John, but Bill's wife just lost her job, and they have three kids in school. I am not sure Bill's family can handle him losing a month's pay. Could we place Bill on final warning, require him to get assistance through the Employee Assistance Program but only give him a week off without pay?" This *F* perspective placed a lot of importance on the personal impact on Bill and his family even though it was not exactly fair. However, the *Ts* in the room got it and they chose the *F* influenced decision. They were concerned about employees seeing it as unfair, but it turned out that Bill and John's coworkers gave management some positive feedback about the decision. The employees knew Bill's family was in a tough financial position and appreciated the company considering that.

I sat in many of those meetings and watched them grapple with the *T/F* difference, and when they fully considered each perspective, they usually made good decisions. Depending on the situation, it might tilt in a *T* or *F* direction.

T/F Impact on Interpersonal Relationships

During my 28 years with Company A, I had the opportunity to get to know a lot of employees in a very personal way. Even though there were approximately 10,000 employees at our site for many of those years, the town in which the site was located had a population of about 45,000 within a region of about 250,000 people. The same people you worked with, you went to church with, your kids attended the same schools, and you socialized with them. As a result, you got to know co-workers very well. As an Employee Assistance Counselor and organizational trainer/consultant, I also worked with a lot of employees on issues of personal growth. This gave me an opportunity to see many people involved in growing and developing as employees and human beings.

Over the years, I had an opportunity to work with one gentleman and watched him move from an individual contributor to a member of the Executive Team. He was a clear *T* and it served him well throughout his career. However, he realized to be successful in management, he would have to be able to understand and influence people. He started a journey that helped him become a role model for influencing others. Two things contributed significantly to his success. Recognizing his need to develop his lesser preferred preference of *Feeling* on the decision-making preference was a big first step. Being intentional about considering the impact of decisions and actions upon people became a part of his thought process. A strong value system relating to caring about people made that thought process an easy step, if not a natural one.

Another key part of his journey in paying attention to what impacted people was being exposed to Stephen Covey's book, *Seven Habits of Highly Effective People*. This individual became a disciple of those habits. He focused a lot of energy on the fifth habit of "seek first to understand, then to be understood." The heart of this habit is gaining an understanding, as much as possible, of where people are and how they see something. This is something people with *Feeling* do more naturally.

Not only did this individual strive to do this in his work and personal relationships, but he did it exceptionally well. It was amazing how it affected his relationships with people and helped him influence decisions in ways that were good for the people involved and what he was trying to accomplish.

The most dramatic example I saw of this was during his first major leadership assignment. Most of his career had been in sales and business roles. In this new assignment, he was given responsibility for a manufacturing division of about nine hundred people. I remember thinking to myself, "They will eat him alive." Company A was in the south and he was from the northeast. Most of the employees he managed were local high school graduates with an operational mindset which at times conflicted with the "guys in suits."

After he had been in this new role for a few months, I started hearing rave reviews from the employees he was managing. They loved him, and they were excited about the things he was doing. I ran into him a few weeks later and told him I was hearing some wonderful things about his leadership from the employees in his division. I then asked him what he thought was the major contributing factor in this positive response. His response was, "Rick, I'm not sure, but I have committed to doing something that I think is really working well." When I asked him what that was, he told me he spends an hour each day with a different group of employees. He did this to get to know them. His intent was to have some time with all nine hundred employees in the division. I asked him what they talked about. He said he asked them the following three questions:

1. How are things at home?
2. How are things at work?
3. Is there anything I can do to make things better for you here?

He then told me how open employees were about the first two questions. He believed it had helped build a personal bond and an important level of trust between him and employees. He also shared it was amazing how many great ideas he got in response to the third question. He indicated he would take those ideas back to his leadership team and they were able to implement many of them. These ideas were improving the results of the division and making things better for employees.

This person with a clear preference for *Thinking* developed his lesser preferred preference of *Feeling* in a way which enhanced his interpersonal relationships at work, at home, and in the community.

T/F Impact on Working Relationships

For about a year with Company A I worked on a company-wide business process improvement effort. My role was change management. We were putting together process improvement teams which had to get up and running quickly. To facilitate an acceleration of team performance, we would do an MBTI team profile and identify issues each team could manage to get to a high performing level in a timely manner. One of the key leaders of this effort had a clear preference for *Thinking* and he did a fantastic job of applying MBTI concepts to leverage his strengths and manage around his potential pitfalls.

After we completed the project, this individual moved into a key business leadership role. It was critical for the team he led to collaborate with other groups to generate sales growth. After a few months in that role, this leader called me and shared that he was in big trouble because he believed everyone on his team had a preference for *Thinking*, and they were alienating everyone with whom they needed to collaborate. After some funny stories and laughter about how much they were like him, we planned an MBTI workshop to help the team better understand the importance of considering how decisions and actions were affecting others.

After reviewing MBTI concepts and information about each of the preferences with the team, we began to look at their team profile. Just as their leader had concluded, they indeed all had a clear preference for *Thinking*. Identifying ways to overcome their lack of the *Feeling* preference became the focus for improving their effectiveness as a team.

The discussion about finding ways to improve was humorous at times because it was really challenging for this very dominant *Thinking* team to get a handle on the *Feeling* preference. Since the lens through which they viewed decisions was strongly *T*, it was difficult to understand how *Fs* approach making decisions. They took it seriously and acknowledged the lack of a *Feeling* perspective explained a lot about why people were not jumping at the opportunity to collaborate with them.

Finally, one young man spoke up and I quote: "Rick, I think the best we're going to be able to do is act like we care." We all laughed, and then I asked them what that would look like if they did. This began a very productive discussion leading to several actions which would improve the working relationships with their business partners. They really did care. They just had to identify ways to express caring in a manner with which this group of clear *Ts* could be comfortable. I later discovered they put a sign on their conference room wall which read: "We act like we care." It worked for them.

T/F Impact on Teamwork

As I mentioned earlier, most management teams are dominated by people with a preference for *Thinking*. On one occasion in Company A, I worked with a manufacturing leadership team with ten members on the team and they were all *Ts*. They were also mostly engineers, so they approached situations from a very logical and analytical viewpoint. They wanted to know the numbers and the evidence on either side of an issue. Part of their success was a product of this analytical process of decision-making. It enabled them to run a division that manufactured complex chemicals in a profitable, safe, and efficient manner. All these results were critical to what this manufacturing division needed to accomplish.

As we looked at their MBTI team profile, I asked them the following question: "Do you all make decisions at times and get blindsided by a negative response to the decision by employees?" They laughed and said, we do that all the time. They also indicated they had difficulty understanding the push back because they believed they had made the right decision. In most cases, they were right, but after a lot of discussion, they acknowledged at times they discovered things about how the decision impacted employees which made them realize the decision needed to be modified in some way or at least communicated differently to address certain employee concerns.

A splendid example of this failure to factor *Feeling* into decisions was a decision requiring employees with beards to immediately shave their beards because their beards prevented their safety masks from getting a tight enough seal in a particular operating area. The manufacturing process in that area had changed such that a chemical could be released which could create health issues if inhaled. Thus, having a tightly sealed mask had just come especially important.

Now to understand the significance of requiring employees to shave their beards, you need to know this chemical plant is in the heart of the southern Appalachian Mountains and beards are an important part of the culture. Many of the employees had a beard their entire adult lives. Their father and grandfather had beards. A beard was a part of their identity. So, when management required employees to shave their beards, it was like taking away a part of who they were. It did not matter that it was unsafe. This requirement created a major negative response from employees.

Management was totally surprised by this reaction. Safety really was the number one focus in these manufacturing areas. They were doing what they felt they had to do to avoid sending these employees home sick to their families. However, the decision did not come across that way to employees, because management failed to reflect an understanding of the importance of wearing a beard to these employees. Management failed to communicate the personal sacrifice they were asking these employees to make.

Looking through the T/F lens helped them see their failure to communicate the change with consideration to the impact on employees. The facts and logic of the decision was the only thing addressed in the communication. The management team realized they needed to reflect an understanding that this was a very personal issue for many employees, and they were sorry it was necessary to require everyone to come to work in that area with a clean-shaven face. The necessity of shaving their beards could not be changed but demonstrating sensitivity about the personal sacrifice they were asking employees to make could have been communicated more effectively.

Management, after considering how much wearing a beard meant for so many employees, decided to give employees an option. If an employee wanted to move to an area of the plant where it was acceptable to wear a beard, they could make that request and every attempt would be made to transfer that employee. It was not a certainty they could move every employee, but management would attempt to accommodate those requests.

By simply communicating the change with more empathy and providing a reasonable alternative for employees to keep their beard, the dissatisfaction about the change reduced significantly. Failing to look at the F perspective created some chaos but looking at the decision again and using some insights gained by viewing the decision more completely improved the decision and deployment of the decision significantly.

Now back to the manufacturing team MBTI workshop. The discussion of situations like the one above led them to put a couple of additional steps into their decision-making process. They added the following questions to their decision-making process: who are the stakeholder groups impacted by this decision; how are those groups affected by this decision; and is there anything we need to do to address that impact? They also recognized that since they were all *Ts*, it might be a challenge to answer that question at times. As a result, they identified some *Fs* within the division who they believed were in tune with employees and other stakeholders. In some situations, they would consult with these employees to get that *F* perspective.

In following up with that team some months later, they indicated those changes in their decision-making process had produced much better decisions, and they were seldom blindsided by the response of employees.

T/F Impact on Organizations

In Company B, caring about people is deeply rooted in their corporate culture. Its parent company had a long history of "taking care of its employees." This concern for people went to a different level in Company B when it conducted an in-depth visioning process. This process defined how they would focus and manage the organization when it became independent of the parent company. This process had multiple stages and spanned a period of several years. A major outcome of this process was the choice of two major corporate measures reflecting the importance of a *T/F* balance in organizational decisions and the way they wanted to operate.

The importance of utilizing the *Thinking* preference in making decisions was reflected in the identification of a critical financial measure. This measure drove their financial engine. Other financial measures were important, but the others were tied to the major measure on which everyone in the organization could focus. The financial and operational engine of the organization ran well when they tied their efforts to this measure which ensured their financial viability and stability.

The attention to the *Feeling* perspective in decisions is evident in their focus on a second measure reflecting how well they serve their members. They see the member as someone with whom they stand. This focus has enabled Company B to achieve an unprecedented level of performance in relation to serving their members. They are relentless in their efforts to meet the needs of their members, and it does not matter if you are the CEO, a teller, a loan officer, the Chief Legal Counsel, or the VP of Human Resources. Employees are told from day one everyone is focused on serving the member, and they quickly learn how their job responsibilities are linked to a measure related to how well they serve their members.

In the early 2,000s, they developed a set of principles to guide every employee's interaction with members. This is not just a document on the wall, but a living set of expectations for every employee. To emphasize the importance of those expectations, they have processes to provide feedback to employees about performance on those expectations. This feedback is used to recognize excellent performance and identify opportunities for improvement.

Company B has observed an interesting relationship between the *T* measure and the *F* measure. They discovered if the measure related to how they serve their members was excellent the financial performance measure was excellent also. These two measures are interdependent. Even the annual bonus system based on these two measures reflects the fairness a *T* wants and the consideration of the personal an *F* considers. Everyone from the CEO to the teller benefits in a fair manner that is good for everyone. Balancing *Thinking* and *Feeling* is as critical in business as it is in our personal lives.

I am not suggesting every decision of Company B is processed through a *Thinking/Feeling* filter. However, their decisions are made in an environment and by people who are very much aware of the realities Carl Jung observed. Just like Jung, they have discovered both logic and impact on people are both important and neglecting either will lead to poorer decisions. Company B also recognizes we naturally consider one of those preferences, and if we do not find a way to consider our lesser preferred preference the quality of our decisions will suffer. MBTI has helped Company B balance these two preferences very well.

Another thing which reflects a *Feeling* consideration in the way they operate is a phrase that is used in Operations, which is the part of the organization that manages branch operations where members are served. The phrase is "every member, every time." As previously mentioned, their motto indicates they stand beside their members. The motto and the guiding phrase in Operations represent a *Feeling* perspective. They are clear about their focus being to assist with the financial needs of their members.

Many financial institutions are moving to online applications and away from personal interactions with customers/members, and many times those decisions are driven by *Thinking* and not *Feeling*. Even though Company B has won awards for some of its online applications, much of this success is driven by the desire expressed by members to have those options. The members still demonstrate a desire for personal service in a branch. If you drive by one of their branches, the parking lot is usually close to full. Operating decisions are about meeting the needs of the member. This is very much an *F* point of view.

Seeing the influence both *Thinking* and *Feeling* have at Company B is not by chance. It is intentional because the leadership has each of these decision-based preferences deeply embedded within the DNA of the organization. Their strategy and goals balance the two. The incentive system of the organization rewards accomplishing goals related to each preference. From employee orientation to their leadership training, all employees learn that total commitment to serving members and relentless pursuit of financial performance is what drives the decisions and behavior of everyone from the CEO to the newest employee.

The importance of maintaining a balance of *Thinking* and *Feeling* can even be seen in the hiring and promotion process. MBTI, as mentioned previously should never be used in organizations for hiring or selection purposes, and it is not by Company B. They use a targeted selection process for hiring people with a major focus on whether an employee will be a good fit with a service minded culture. Demonstrating a service mentality is a major factor in determining promotions into leadership positions. If you do not show your commitment to serving members and an ability to collaborate with others in serving members, you will not advance in Company B.

In most financial institutions, if you looked at the MBTI profile for their leadership, a high percentage of their management would have a preference for *Thinking*. In company B, their management council includes approximately eighty leaders. The distribution on *Thinking* and *Feeling* is about half and half. This is unusual for any leadership group and particularly in the financial sector which is normally dominated by the *Thinking* preference.

This balance of *T/F* demonstrates both *Thinking* and *Feeling* perspectives are given equal value in this organization, and their top management believes this is a key to their success.

- **What:** Balancing *Thinking* and *Feeling* in our life decisions is critical.
- **So What:** If we do not consider the T and F components of decisions, we will miss something which needs to be considered in making the best decision.
- **Now What:** To make the best decisions we need to ask, what does the evidence suggest is the most logical thing to do and how are people involved in this decision impacted. Once we answer those two questions, then we can balance the logic and impact on people to arrive at the optimal decision.

CHAPTER 7

INFLUENCE OF THE JUDGING/PERCEIVING (J/P) PREFERENCE

As previously mentioned, this is the preference Isabella Myers and Katherine Briggs added. The preference addresses the issue of what we are doing in relation to the world around us. During every waking hour, we are either *Perceiving* or *Judging* the world around us. When we are *Perceiving* the world, we are observing the world either through our five senses or through the lens of hunches and possibilities. We are gathering information about what is going on "out there." When we are *Judging* the world, we are organizing it, acting upon it, or making decisions about what is going on around us. We process that information either through logic and reason or how people are being affected.

Having worked with MBTI for over forty years, I have grown to believe this might be the most influential preference. We all use both preferences, but our preference for one over the other will tell us where we invest most of our attention and this has a significant impact on the way we approach everything in our lives. Let me try to explain this belief.

People with a preference for *Judging* go through life observing something and then quickly drawing a conclusion or taking action to do something about it. They want to make a decision whether it is good, bad, right, or wrong. They want to organize or clean up what they have observed so it is not the mess it currently is. They have a strong bias for action, so they want to decide what needs to be done, make a list and start checking things off that list. At times, they will realize they acted too soon and should have gathered more information through use of the *Perceiving* preference, but this not where they prefer to operate. They want to get it done, not watch it happen. They want to act and move on to the next thing.

People with a preference for *Perceiving*, on the other hand, go through life observing the world around them, and instead of quickly jumping to judging, they observe some more. Because of their curiosity and desire to gather more information, they want to take everything in because their fulfillment comes from understanding and not from acting. They only move to the use of *Judging* when they see the need for action because of the understanding they have gained or when someone else initiates action.

Whether two people are spouses, friends, co-workers, or manager/employee, it can be challenging when one person is in *Judging* mode and the other is immersed in *Perceiving*. The *Judging* person will tend to become frustrated because for them it is obvious some action needs to be taken. At the same time, the *Perceiving* person is still taking in information which they believe is important and needs to be considered. The *Judging* person might tend to see the Perceiving person as a procrastinator and someone who is lazy and not willing to get things done. The *Perceiving* person may see the *Judging* person as someone who moves too quickly without fully considering all the relevant information or too quick to draw conclusions and make judgments without adequate information. If these natural preferences are not understood and appreciated, major problems can arise.

On the other hand, when understood and valued, this difference can be a major source of synergy and effectiveness. To illustrate, I will use my relationship with my mentor, Zellie. Zellie had a clear preference for *Judging,* and I have a clear preference for *Perceiving.* At times, this difference frustrated him and at times it was frustrating for me. However, we learned to use it to our advantage. We would do major teambuilding events or leadership retreats which required months of preparation. After we developed the basic design for these events, we would identify the actions that needed to be completed to ensure we were ready for the event. Zellie wanted to get them all done immediately. We found it was best to divide preparation into three buckets. One was his to-do list that he would attack. The second was a to-do list that required both of us and we would tackle that together. Then the final list was a little less defined and required more information. That was my work which I would take on in my own way. It always got done but not in the way Zellie would have done it. On those activities, a *Perceiving* approach worked better.

My favorite story about the way *J/P* preferences influence every situation occurred during a community leadership retreat we did together. We were starting the retreat with a MBTI workshop. Zellie was going to do the introduction and talk about *E/I.* I would then talk about *S/N,* and he would then cover *T/F.* I would then finish with *J/P* and close out the workshop. We arrived at the venue about 30 minutes before the participants and our classroom was a large room with thirty-four chairs around tables in a U shape. At the front of the room were a screen and an overhead projector (1990 technology) which used transparent slides. The projector was on a tall table, and there was room for only one notebook of slides on the table.

Zellie had his slides in a notebook, and I had mine. This lack of space for two notebooks threw this *Judging* person into panic mode. He looked at me and said: "Rick, there is not room for both of our notebooks, and it will be distracting to carry our notebooks back and forth. What are we going to do?" He wanted to try to get another table or figure out some complex solution for which we did not have the time. I said "Zellie, why don't we just both use your notebook?" He was surprised because he could not understand how I could use his notebook. I reassured him I was familiar with his slides and had no problem using them. Adapting is easy for someone with a preference for *Perceiving*. He thanked me and indicated this would make it much easier for him. I knew how important going with the plan was to Zellie.

An additional humorous illustration of the *J/P* difference occurred during the workshop. I did not notice it or think about it, but when Zellie started the workshop and did the first segment, he took his slides out of the rings in his notebook and put them back into the rings before he reached for another slide. This is very typical of an organized *Judging* person. When I got up to talk about *S/N*, without even thinking, I would take a slide out and after discussing it would just simply lay the slide on the notebook and reach for another slide. When I finished covering *S/N*, Zellie came up to talk about *T/F*. Before he began, he took all my slides, straightened them up, and put them back into the rings in the notebook. Knowing I would be talking about *J/P*, I thought this is just too good an illustration of the *J/P* difference. When I started my review of *J/P* and finished discussing the first slide, instead of placing the slide on the notebook I tossed it and it hit the notebook and went off onto the floor. Zellie was behind me, and you could hear this "huh." I then asked the class if they heard the "huh." I told them Zellie really wanted to say: "why don't you put that transparency back in the binder." We all had a good laugh at this *J*'s frustration with his *P* friend.

This preference is operating every waking hour and understanding it can help us in many situations.

J/P Impact on Interpersonal Relationships

A young couple came to me indicating they were having some difficulties in their relationship. As they described those challenges, it became obvious they had a *J/P* issue. They had a good relationship. Communication was good, and they shared the same values and a lot of the same interests and loved each other very much. However, they were experiencing some major irritations with one another and were having difficulty resolving the issue.

I asked them to take the MBTI and it confirmed the husband was a clear *J*, and the wife was a *P*. He was as organized an individual as I had ever encountered. Everything had to be in its place, and he had a strict system for that. For example, his closet had slacks organized from dark to light, and they had to be hung in a very particular way. His shirts were then hung together from dark to light, and they were buttoned up in a specific way. His shoes were organized on racks. His closet was extremely organized, and he wanted the rest of his space to have the same order. He also had a strict sequence of doing things and did not like to deviate from the plan. Once a decision was made or a plan was developed, he expected everything to go as scheduled.

The wife was much more laid back and open to things changing as you went along. She saw change and adapting as part of life. She was not disturbed if things changed in mid-stream or if you changed your mind. In terms of organizing her life, she was not as particular or systematic in the way she wanted things to be around her. Her closet was not a major mess, but things were not hanging in any order, and the shoes were on the floor of the closet and not always in pairs. She was fine if there was some clutter in the rest of her space. She knew where everything was and did not find it that difficult to locate something.

The lack of organization, structure, and closure in various areas of their relationship was driving him crazy. The push for everything being in a particular place was becoming irritating for her. She was having a challenging time accepting and conforming to his expectations, and he felt like she was not considerate of his desire for more order in their shared life.

By looking at their *J/P* difference, they were able to make it less personal and more about natural and understandable differences in the way they preferred to invest their attention each day. He began to demand less of her in terms of doing things the way he liked them. He also accepted a part of their life being a little less organized than he would like it to be. She began to recognize it was important to invest a little more energy in doing things a specific way when it had a significant impact on him. She began to see providing more structure as simply being respectful of his preference.

Most importantly, they began to really value what the other brought to the relationship and realized how they complemented each other in some important ways. She recognized life needs structure, and he brought that to their relationship. She depended on him for the organization they needed. He recognized his difficulty adapting when things did not go as planned, and he depended on her to find a way to make things work when the plan failed. Instead of resenting the differences in each other, they came to value what the other brought to the relationship.

J/P Impact on Working Relationships

I recall a good working relationship that could have been quite a challenge. She was an *ISTJ*, and I am an *ENFP*. We were opposite on all four preferences. We saw the world very differently and functioned in the world in diverse ways. Fortunately, we knew about those differences and made every effort to respect and value those differences. The *J/P* difference was the one that we learned to appreciate the most.

We worked together on a few significant projects. At the beginning of those projects, we would get together and develop a project plan. This was at her request, and as a *J*, beginning with a plan is what you would expect her to do. As we would develop that plan, we would consider MBTI and particularly our *J* and *P* as we assigned those responsibilities. She loved and wanted all the logistical, specific, and time sequenced activities because she would develop her list and check those things off. This brought her a great deal of satisfaction, and she was good at getting things done. The activities which were less specific and dependent on things that might happen over the course of the project or required gathering more input were things I was assigned. The ambiguity or uncertainty of those activities was not a problem for me, and in fact, I found them invigorating. She would look at my assignments and say: "Thank goodness I don't have to do those things." I felt the same way about her assignments.

By playing to our preferences and our strengths, we were able to do the things each did best and the things that we enjoyed most. I was not taking advantage of her nor her of me. The project was completed successfully, and it was a much more satisfying and rewarding experience for both of us. We grew to have a great deal of trust in each other. She knew I would do the parts of the project that fit my strengths in my way, and I knew she would do her part of the project that better fit her strengths in her way. The projects were done well, and we loved working together. This was a mutually beneficial win-win outcome.

J/P Impact on Teamwork

While doing some teambuilding work with a manufacturing team, we did an MBTI team profile. Their profile showed all members of this nine-member team were Js. As we looked at the characteristics of Js, they confirmed those characteristics described their team very well, and they shared some funny stories about the extremes to which they would go to ensure everything was done "in turn and in order."

As we talked about how their J was a strength, particularly in manufacturing, I asked them if, at times, they made decisions and then later discovered something which created problems with those decisions. They indicated this was not unusual. We discussed how being an all

J-team created a strong bias for decisiveness and action which served them well in most circumstances. However, we discussed how it could result in them making some decisions too quickly to move on to the next item. They recognized the benefits of exploring some decisions more thoroughly and in some cases gathering more input from outside the team.

One of their improvement actions they began taking was to ask the following questions when their team faced significant decisions: when do we have to make this decision, and who will be responsible for gathering more information related to the decision and providing that information to the team? In response to those questions, they would place the decision on a later agenda and assign one person to be primarily responsible for gathering and sharing relevant information related to the decision. Everyone, of course, was responsible for giving the question more thought prior to the meeting at which they would make the decision.

I followed up with the team months later to see how the changes in their decision-making process were working. The division head indicated the team believed the quality of their decisions had improved significantly, and they were not getting blindsided later by information they had not considered.

J/P Impact on Organizations

I have worked with Company B for 16 years, and all the employees eventually go through an MBTI workshop. The workshop helps them gain a basic understanding of the concepts related to personality types and preferences and identify ways to apply that understanding to their working relationships with co-workers and their interaction with members. As I began compiling MBTI preferences and types for their employees, I observed two major trends when comparing their employee population to the general population. They tended to have more *F* employees than the general population. This was understandable since they had a higher percentage of females in their employee population than the general population and about 65% of females are *F* on the *T/F* preference. It could also have been influenced by the fact Company B places so much attention on serving members and developing strong employee relationships. Company B hires people who have a strong service mindset. *Fs* would be naturally drawn to this type of work culture.

The second trend I observed was the high percentage of *Judging* in the employee population. Company B had a much higher percentage of *Judging* than the general population. As I began to observe this pattern, I shared the information with the VP of Human Resources, and we discussed whether this higher percentage of the *Judging* preference in Company B made sense considering the nature of Company B's business. As a financial institution, we concluded having a higher percentage of *Js* made sense. Financial institutions are highly regulated and have strict and well-defined processes for operating. They need people who are effective and comfortable working in that type of highly structured environment and people who have the *J* preference would be a good fit.

We also discussed how the targeted selection process was designed to find employees who would be effective working in a structured environment. The high percentage of employees with the preference for *J* was in some ways a validation that the targeted selection process was selecting employees who would be a good fit for the type of work Company B did.

This conversation with the VP of HR and then other members of senior leadership began a dialogue about how to best manage this *J* dominance. They wanted to ensure it did not become a potential pitfall. One way too much *Judging* and not enough *Perceiving* could create problems would be for the organization to lack flexibility when needed. Management assessed whether they were adaptive and willing to change when change was needed. We will look at a few things Company B does to build adaptability and flexibility into a corporate culture which might not naturally have those characteristics.

All managers go through two 4-day leadership development courses. Each of those courses has a module on change management. The first course explores the inevitability of change and transition in the workplace and considers how change impacts employees. The training shares ways to coach and help employees through change with the goal of minimizing the personal stress for them and increasing the probability the change will be successful for the company.

The second course looks at how to lead groups of people through transitions by having good change management practices. In this material, we talk about the following: providing a compelling case for why the change is in the best interest of the employees and the company; defining a clear vision of where the change will lead us; providing a clear plan for the things that will lead to a successful change; ensuring leadership is on board with the change; communicating continuously through the change; and celebrating when you have successfully achieved the desired change.

By building the capability of all leaders to help employees and the organization to deal with change, we are building organizational adaptability. People with a preference for *P* are naturally adaptable. By being intentional in teaching people ways to be adaptable, we can improve the flexibility of an organization dominated by *J*s.

At an organizational management level, one process that Company B utilizes as well as any organization is scenario planning. The definition of scenario planning includes the following: a strategic planning process used to create flexible long-term plans. Many organizations get locked into a plan based on certain assumptions, and when those assumptions do not prove to be true, these organizations find themselves scrambling to adjust. Scenario planning involves developing plans based on different assumptions so you will be prepared to adapt when a change of direction is needed.

I believe this organization's understanding of the value of all MBTI preferences has contributed to their excellence in scenario planning. They as a natural *J* organization are exceptional at developing and executing plans. I have seen some strongly *J* organizations have a challenging time accepting the fact their plan is not working and there is a need to adapt and move in a different direction. Scenario planning has enabled Company B to develop a great deal of adaptability because it is part of their planning process.

One additional factor has contributed to the dominant *J* not becoming problematic for Company B. The senior leadership of this organization have a wonderful grasp of the way MBTI influences our decisions and behaviors. They use it to understand and inform situations that occur each day. I have often heard them acknowledge how a decision or plan did not work. They then utilize what they have learned to guide future decisions and actions. Humility is critical in using MBTI effectively because we all have strengths and weaknesses. I can never compensate for my weaknesses unless I own them. Many organizations are not willing to confront the brutal facts. Things do not always go as planned and it is critical to have the ability to adjust to that failure. The leaders and employees of Company B know the strengths and pitfalls associated with each preference. They utilize that knowledge to help them adapt when their preference may not be achieving the desired results.

- **What:** *Judging* and *Perceiving* impacts how we approach every situation of life.
- **So What:** The daily activities of life present situations involving either *Judging* activities like organizing and making a decision about something or *Perceiving* activities like adapting to a situation or taking in more information. Understanding how our natural preferences fit some of the situations well and others not so well is important to our effectiveness.

- **Now What:** I will seek out situations where my natural J/P preference works well and develop my lesser preferred preference or seek out others or processes to assist me in situations where my natural preference does not work.

Op-Ed on Use of Non-preferred Preference

In many stories I have shared ways to help better understand how the preferences influence our decisions and actions. I have shared how individuals, teams and even organizations have learned to: develop their lesser preferred preference over time; compensate for weaknesses associated with their preferences by doing things with intentionality; and/or, find others to help them with their non-preferred preferences. It is important for an *Extravert* to stop and reflect at times. An *Introvert* at times needs to get their ideas out into the external world to be effective. Some situations in life require a *Sensing* person to stop hanging onto the past and embrace the future. People who have a preference for *Intuition* need to consider how the practical realities of a situation might make their hunch impossible to pursue. *Thinking* people need to recognize that sometimes the concerns of people will overwhelm the logic of the decision. *Feeling* people must realize there are rational factors in many decisions which make it impossible to please everyone.

Using the other preference is hard if we have a clear preference for the opposite preference, but life is hard at times. Jung recognized a major dimension of maturity is learning to use the opposite preference even though it is not natural or easy. We need to be aware that at times we encounter things in life where we do not need to depend only on what is natural and what we are best at doing. At times, we need to use the other hand. We can do this through practice, with help from others, and utilizing processes or tools to help us.

This is even more critical as we consider the *J/P* preference. Remember, we are using one of these preferences every moment of every day.

We are either: making decisions, organizing our ideas or things in the world, and acting on something with the intention of completing the task; or, observing the world around us, seeking to understand something, discovering something new, and adjusting to a changing environment. Our *J/P* preference determines which of those areas receive most of our attention.

I have seen a lot of people with a preference for *Judging* get things done which had to be redone and drawing conclusions which were ill-informed, because they jumped to conclusions without gathering enough information. On the other hand, I have seen so many people with a preference for *Perceiving* miss opportunities because they did not recognize the need to act. They stayed in the gathering of information mode until it was too late to act on something which could have benefited them and others.

I believe recognizing the need to utilize our lesser preferred *J/P* preference at certain points in our lives is a key success factor in life. I want to share two situations where leaders had a sense for the need to do this and took actions either consciously or unconsciously to make sure there was a good balance between the *J* and *P*.

Over a period of 13 years, I worked with a small company of about one hundred employees, and they had a real estate development company, a construction company, and a property management company. The primary focus of my work with them was strategic and annual business planning. As a part of that work, we did MBTI in about the third year with all the employees who participated in the annual planning process.

When I got the MBTI results, it included about forty-four employees, and I was amazed at the results. I had already been able to observe some interesting dynamics within the company. The owner/CEO was in his early thirties and had taken over the leadership of the company from his father. The owner/CEO was an *ENTP* and was a visionary and dynamic leader. The company had grown significantly under his leadership. Much of the growth was due to his creativity, willingness to tackle a lot of new things, and ability to find a way to overcome any barriers. It was interesting that the forty-three other employees were all Js. When I got the results, I contacted the owner/CEO and shared with him that he had balanced his extreme P with a group of J employees. He was the change agent, explorer of all possibilities, and researcher of all the things that touched their businesses. He surrounded himself unconsciously with people who could implement his ideas and provide the structure needed.

My second example is a senior leader who led a part of an organization that included about 3,000 employees and over $3B of business. This leader led a high performing J team which had a strong bias for action. They placed a high priority on treating employees well, but their strong business focus and the fact they were all Ts resulted in them making decisions at times without fully considering the impact of those decisions upon employees. I was the facilitator for this leadership team. In addition, I am an F with a psychology and ministerial background. This senior leader wanted me to focus on "observing them do their work and let them know before they screwed something up in relation to people." In other words, he wanted me to use my P to help them compensate for their very dominant J. That is what I did, and it worked. In addition, it was rewarding for me. They recognized the value I brought to the team because they understood MBTI and knew the strengths and pitfalls of each preference. When I shared those people concerns with them, I also had a deep respect both for their T perspective and the need to move on at times driven by their J and the situation. It was less about right or wrong and more about understanding the need to consider all perspectives.

CHAPTER 8

THE IN/EN/ES/IS DYNAMIC

In the next two chapters I would like to explore the dynamics when you combine pairs of preferences. We will not pull the pairs out of the air but there will be some rationale for the pairs discussed.

The most recognized work related to pairs of MBTI preferences was done by Dr. David Keirsey and Marilyn Bates (1984) and is described beautifully in their book, *Please Understand Me: Character and Temperament Types*. They describe combining preferences in a manner which produces what they define as four temperaments. Keirsey applied MBTI concepts to the ancient study of temperaments by Hippocrates and Plato. He used the names that Plato used for temperaments. The four temperaments he described using MBTI were:

- **Artisans (SP):** They are concrete and adaptable and are exceptional at troubleshooting and fixing things.
- **Guardians (SJ):** They are concrete and organized and excel at keeping things running in an orderly manner.
- **Idealists (NF):** They are abstract and compassionate and are concerned with things like meaning, personal growth and helping others work together.

- **Rationals (NT):** They are abstract and objective and are exceptional at arranging things in a connected them effective manner and inventing new things.

Keirsey has authored many other books on the topic of temperaments. I will not explore temperaments because I could not add to his work, and I have not used temperaments much in the work I have done over the years.

The first pairs of preferences I used extensively over the years are the combinations you get when you combine the *E/I* preference with the *S/N* preference. When you look at the four possible combinations of these preferences, they end up being the first two letters of the four types in each quadrant of the MBTI type table shown below:

ISTJ	ISFJ	INFJ	INTJ
ISTP	ISFP	INFP	INTP
ESTP	ESFP	ENFP	ENTP
ESTJ	ESFJ	ENFJ	ENTJ

By looking at the individual preferences, combinations of letters, and the four-letter types, you can gain insights about how our personality intersects with the things we do as we go about each day.

The first time I came across the four-quadrant model with the *E/I* and *S/N* preferences was in a booklet called, *Introduction to Type and Teams*, by Elizabeth Hirsh, Katherine W. Hirsh, and Sandra Krebs

Hirsh (2003). Their work led me to experiment with the concepts flowing from this model and learn from others who were using it.

As I worked with the model, I realized it explained so much about what I had observed with organizations as they navigated notable change. It helped me understand how I functioned in relation to change and how others dealt with change in diverse ways. It also enabled me to see mistakes I had made by being too impulsive at times and too quick to jump into something new which is very natural for *ENs* to do. It helped me understand my frustration with *ISs* who seemed slow and even resistant to change. As I have mentioned before, Carl Jung's concepts as measured by MBTI are so practical in describing our life journey, and this quadrant lens is important in helping us navigate the inevitable changes of life.

In the table on the next page, we will examine the quadrants that include the following four pairs of preferences: *IN/EN/ES/IN.* We will also explore a brief description of each and what implications they have for a relationship, team, and organization. As you review the table, start with the *IN,* and go clockwise because it best describes the value each of the four pairs brings to the stages of change.

IS	IN
ISs are the stabilizing force, and their motto is "let's keep it." Their philosophy is "if it isn't broke, why fix it." They are not impulsive, and they are highly invested in keeping things running smoothly. They are the ones who know the history that brought us to this point, and why it is important to maintain the status quo. They can be resistant to change and need to be brought along to embrace something new.	INs are the "idea" people, and their motto is "let us think about it differently." They generate ideas that have not been thought of and might seem unrealistic. You need to be careful about rejecting their ideas because every idea might not be realistic nor a breakthrough, but one clever idea could dramatically improve the organization/team. They think deeply and in very innovative ways. These are the Bill Gates of the world.
ES	**EN**
ESs are the builders of the world, and their motto is "let's do it." They love bringing practical things into reality in the external world. They are active and love to have a project to work on. They love seeing something come into existence that meets a practical need. Sometimes they can get so focused on acting that they fail to see the big picture or question what we are creating. Their strength is building, not maintaining.	ENs are the creators of change, and their motto is "let's change it." These are the change agents of the world. They are quick to embrace innovative ideas and begin actively to pursue making the change. They are often visionary in seeing how the innovative ideas generated can become a reality. They have a tough time diving into the necessary details needed to make the change a reality.

The characteristics of these pairs are important to understand both as an individual and particularly when you are part of a team. If you think about a model for how change works, it really is described beautifully by these pairs of preferences. If you think about change, it goes through the following steps:

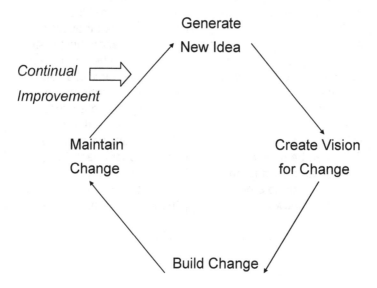

We move through life living in a reality that we understand and accept as the current state or norm. Then someone produces a breakthrough idea like an iPhone, and someone embraces that change and creates a vision for it and then someone builds the actual iPhone, and our world becomes a new reality. We have been living in that reality for the last 15 years and it is difficult to imagine functioning without this piece of technology. Someday there will be a new idea which will bring about changes which will make the iPhone obsolete.

Understanding this process is so important in life. I am an *EN*. As a result, I love change and enjoy being a part of making change happen. A major part of my role during the latter part of my career with Company A was working with leadership to plan and manage the human component of major change efforts. It was one of the most rewarding periods of my career because it was a wonderful fit for my natural gifts. I can contrast that with the first three years I worked with Company A after graduating from college. My role was primarily wage and salary administration. We were perceived as guardians of the human resource procedures. It was all about "knowing the rules" and making sure everyone abided by the rules. Many of the people who loved that work were ISs, and it was a great fit for them. For them, life was about "let's keep it." The "let's change it" mindset of my EN was not a good fit, and it was a struggle for those three years. I worked with great people, and the company was excellent. However, the nature of the work did not fit me, and that poor fit was part of the reason I left the company. That significant career change enabled me to move into a series of jobs which were a wonderful fit for my personality.

Individually, it is important to understand what your pair of preferences suggests about the way you respond in situations. If I am an IS, I must recognize the importance of being open to new ideas and be willing to embark upon a change and create something new at times. If I am an ES, I must also recognize the importance of being open to innovative ideas and be willing to embark upon a change while also realizing that some things might not need to change. If I am an EN, I need to be open to innovative ideas but also realize changes need to be built in a way that is sustainable and some things do not need to be changed. If I am an IN, I need to realize it is not sufficient for a change to be conceptual. For change to be of value, it must be embarked upon, constructed, and become operational.

It is important to understand which of the four "sandboxes" I enjoy and function in best. This will enable me to make my optimal contribution. I will increase my effectiveness, both individually and in working with others, when I value the perspective each of the other three "sandboxes" bring. This understanding will increase my ability to help translate ideas into changes which will produce sustained value over time.

This model for how change can translate ideas into things of substantial value is of great benefit for teams. When I do MBTI teambuilding workshops, we always look at the make-up of the team in relation to these four pairs of preferences. It is so interesting how the team distribution for these pairs often fit the nature of that team's work. For example, when I did workshops with research and development groups, most of the team members were in the *IN* quadrant, because their job is generating new models related to molecules or products. If I was working with a marketing group, most of them were *EN*s because their work is creating ideas and getting folks excited about something new. When I worked with engineering and construction, most of the group tended to be *ES*s because they were about putting concrete in the ground and building things. When I worked with manufacturing teams, most of the team would be *IS*s because they were about running that plant safely and without interruption day in and day out.

In working with teams, it was important to consider how their work fit with their *IS/ES/EN/IN* profile. Secondly, we would examine how their profile might point to any issues they needed to manage as a team. For example, if a team did not have any *ES*s, we would determine if that presented a problem in translating ideas into reality. If it did, we would consider what they could do to compensate for this natural weakness. It could result in them developing some good project management skills as a team or getting assistance from outside their team if needed.

Carl Jung described the basic patterns of human behavior which operate in our day-to-day life experiences. These paired combinations are so descriptive of the way life works in relation to the changes of life. Understanding how we and others function in relation to the change process is invaluable in helping to navigate that process.

- **What:** The *IN/EN/ES/IS* pairs of preferences portray how a new idea is generated, energized into change, implemented into reality, and sustained over time to realize the benefit of the change.

- **So What:** By understanding this change process and the strengths and potential pitfalls associated with my pair of preferences, I can better move through those steps and help others do the same.
- **Now What:** I will value each of the steps in the change process and be intentional about choosing whether to change or not and identify what needs to be done to successfully bring about needed change.

CHAPTER 9

THE SJ/SP/NP/NJ DYNAMIC

There are two correlations between MBTI preferences. If you are *Sensing*, you are more likely to be *Judging*, and if you are *Intuition*, you are more likely to be *Perceiving*. Like many other MBTI concepts, this correlation makes sense. If you are *Sensing*, it is so much easier to be *Judging*. It is important for people with a preference for *J* to complete things and for things to go as planned. If you are a *J*, having a preference also for *S* makes things much easier because as an *S* you are practical and realistic. You do not bite off more than you can chew. You will only use your *J* to plan the things you know you can complete. If someone wants you to do more, you will simply respond with "no we don't have time to do all those things." You keep life simple by not scheduling more than you know you can finish. If a *SJ* plans to do two things on Saturday, they will do those two things. Do not try to get them to do a third thing. It will not happen.

The other correlation of *Intuition* with *Perceiving* is also natural. *Intuitives* are idea and activity generators. They love to generate all kinds of things to do. If *Ns* are also *Ps*, this makes life much easier, because for a *P* life is more about starting things and moving from one thing to another. So, if an *NP* does not finish all those things they start, that is OK. The *NPs* do the things that seem the most important and do not worry about the things left undone. They may plan five things to do this Saturday and they will do two things, but they are OK with that because they are not driven to finish things.

As you can see, the correlated preferences fit naturally so the correlation is easy to understand. When you combine the preferences which are not correlated, you get some interesting dynamics. For example, if you combine the *Sensing* with *Perceiving*, you get someone who is very practical and realistic in addition to someone who is laid-back and not driven by completing things. They are the ultimate adapters. They live in the moment and are quite comfortable adjusting to change and dropping what they are doing for something different. These are my favorite people in the world because they are easy going and love to play. They are not likely to have a heart attack. They do not live by the world's agenda. Going with the flow is perfectly acceptable to them. They are the ultimate trouble-shooters who can find ways to adjust when things do not work out. They find a way to fix things in a practical manner. They may plan two things for Saturday, but if something better comes up, they are fine dropping the other two things and doing the new and more attractive option.

The final combination is *Intuition* and *Judging*. Ns generate many ideas and activities they want to pursue, and when they are Js, they are driven to finish every idea or activity they start. They, as a result, plan five things for Saturday and feel compelled to complete all five. Lacking the practical S, they do not complete all five activities unless they drive themselves or others beyond reasonable limits. This can either create significant stress for them or a sense of failure if they are unable to complete every activity. I have worked with a lot of NJs over the years and they are often high performers and in fact many top executives are NJs. For NJs, it is important to learn to be graceful toward themselves. It is so important to focus on what they accomplish and be realistic about what they do not complete. This is where having a good S friend or colleague is important to help them understand what is realistic.

The most dramatic example I have observed to demonstrate the way these different combinations can help each other was the dynamics I observed with a senior leadership team. The team had a strong *NJ* leader and most of the members of the team were *NJs*. The organization they led was experiencing an incredible amount of change including several acquisitions, building multiple manufacturing sites around the world, implementation of a new information system that was organizational wide, and significant cost pressures on existing businesses. Employees in the organization felt overwhelmed and were pushing back against an endless wave of initiatives. The senior leader's favorite response to this employee concern was a view shared by a consultant who worked with the organization. That viewpoint was: "You are never limited by resources, only your lack of creativity." This rang true for the *NJ* leader, but most of the employees in the organization were *SJs* and *SPs*, and they were seeing the problems associated with not having adequate people and other resources to carry out all the initiatives.

In addition, the major *SJ* influence on the leadership team was the equivalent of the chief operational officer of the company. He led an operations team responsible for guiding execution of all those initiatives. His background, skill set, and personality were perfect for this role. He was an *ESTJ*. He was an implementer and was driven by getting things done and he loved a challenge. But he was also a realist, and he heard what the employees were saying. The *ESTJ* leader's efforts to raise real resource issues and limit the number of new initiatives were not successful.

During that time, I would do an MBTI workshop with this leadership team about every two years, and we would look at the team profile and how their profile might be impacting their working relationship and the work they were doing. During the workshop I shared how during this time of heavy work demands, their dominance of *NJ* on the team might create excessive demands on the organization and they might consider taking a stronger *SJ* perspective at times. There was an intellectual acceptance that this could be true. However, I sensed nothing would change. I have often wondered whether the performance of the company was affected by the challenge in balancing the NJ and SJ perspective.

This situation demonstrated there is not a right or wrong approach when we look at the pairs of SJ/SP/NP/NJ. They all bring something of value and can be useful in guiding us at times. In the situation we just reviewed, it would have helped if the NJs could have seen the value of the SJ perspective. Better decisions would have been made if the SJs could have been more effective in influencing the NJs to give more consideration to resources as they explore more initiatives. If the NJ and SJ could have been better balanced, it could have had a significant impact on the performance of the organization and the results they achieved.

I would like to share what each of the SJ/SP/NP/NJ pairs of preferences bring to the table. I will draw on some Biblical characters to illustrate what each pair looks like. For one pair, I will use two giants of the Christian faith, Peter, and Paul. For the other pair, I will use two ladies, Mary, and Martha. These ladies hosted Jesus in their home. To predict their type, I will use my impressions from stories my mom told in Sunday School with a story board of felt characters and years of studying and teaching the Bible.

We will use Peter and Paul to contrast the very opposite pairs of SP and NJ. I believe Peter was an SP. As a fisherman, Peter was in a practical and hands-on job. It is important to be in touch with temperature, feeding locations, what bait works best in each situation, and other important sensory data. The name Jesus gave Peter meant "rock," so Jesus saw him as someone who was solid and easy to see and touch. Peter seemed to live in the moment and was a keen observer of the world around him. It is easy to see him as being *Sensing*. People with a preference for *Sensing* find it difficult at times to embrace something radically new. Peter found it difficult to grasp that Jesus came as a Savior and Lord for all people and not simply as the Messiah to the

Jewish people like him. He seems to have believed you had to become a Jewish believer first and then act on your belief in Jesus. Despite walking with Jesus and seeing him break down the barriers between Jew and non-Jew in his teachings and actions, Peter had a tough time breaking with his Jewish traditions. Not until Acts 11 do we see Peter express an understanding that a relationship with Jesus was not conditioned on embracing the traditions of the Jewish faith.

Peter was a rock and provided a key link for Christianity with its Jewish roots, but he was adaptable enough to change when Jesus' teachings finally sank in, and he began to see it being lived out in the lives of Gentile believers. His *SP* strength served him well in carrying out what Jesus called him to do.

I believe Peter was also *Perceiving* because his life was very adaptable in many ways. Certainly, as a fisherman you need to be able to adjust to changing conditions to be able to maximize your catch. Peter also was very spontaneous in responding to the events he encountered. He never seemed locked into a plan.

Paul on the other hand seems to be an *NJ*. I believe Paul was called as an apostle because none of the original disciples seemed to fully grasp God's vision for the church and the growth of Christianity outside the Jewish faith. Despite being a very devout Jew, Paul persecuted early Christians for deviating from the Jewish faith and embracing Jesus as the Messiah. Once Paul encountered Jesus on the road to Damascus, he became known as the apostle to the non-Jew and began starting churches all over the known world of that day. For the 30 years following his conversion to Christianity, he started 14-20 churches in Rome, Greece, today's Western Europe and Asia Minor. Paul embraced change and became a visionary who helped spread Christianity in an unbelievable manner. As I write this, the world is experiencing the Coronavirus pandemic. On March 1, there were three cases of the virus reported in the United States. Two months later, there were over a million cases. This rate of spread is incredible. Today there are 2.4 billion Christians in every country in the world. In about 2,000 years Christianity grew from a handful of people to be one of the major influences in our world. Paul had more to do with that incredible spread of Christianity than any other human being.

Paul saw possibilities that no one could really envision and that sounds like an N to me. I believe he also had a preference for *Judging* because he did not just "wing it." He organized his efforts in a very strategic way. He realized he could not do it on his own, so he mentored several people like Barnabus, Silas, Timothy, Epaphras, and others. He understood the concept of multiplication, so he developed others to go out and do the same things he was doing. Secondly, he went to the major cities of influence like Rome and centers of trade like Antioch. These were centers for large populations, but they were also places where people from all over the world would come and go. This meant the Christian faith could touch the lives of more people and spread like a pandemic, and it did. This type of visionary leadership is common for NJs and in Paul it was essential for his calling.

To illustrate the contrast between the *SJ* and the *NP* pairs I would like to use the sisters Mary and Martha who we encounter in Luke 10:38-42. In this brief but eventful story, we see them hosting Jesus and his disciples as they were traveling. These sisters were obviously excited about Jesus' visit because Martha begins scurrying about with preparations to host and feed them. Mary on the other hand positioned herself at Jesus' feet as Jesus shared with the disciples, Lazarus, and others. Martha points out to Jesus that Mary is not helping and asks Jesus to tell Mary to help her. Jesus tells Martha she worries and gets upset about too many things. He also tells her only one thing is needed, and Mary has chosen the more important thing. Mary knew she was in the presence of someone special who had transformational thoughts to share. She also realized she might never have another opportunity to share time with Jesus.

I believe Martha was an *SJ* and so much about being an *SJ* is good. Their *Sensing* enables them to be to be in touch with real world issues. They are practical and pay attention to the things that need to be done each day. They will help a neighbor by bringing a meal over when they are sick, because they know certain practical things need to be done. And as a *J*, the *SJ* will also get it done. They will put those daily activities on their list and will systematically check them off the list. *SJs* are those folks who keep the world running day in and day out.

The major shortcoming for *SJs* is they occasionally miss the special moments in life or the unique opportunities which come and go in an instant. They will occasionally miss something special because they are so driven to get the things on their list done. Unfortunately, many of these special things happen in a moment which cannot be recaptured. Those items on the list may be of much less importance. One of the most profound songs about being a father ever written was "Cats in the Cradle" by Harry Chapin. A line which captures the danger of always being driven by our to-do list is the response of the father when his son asked him to teach him to throw: "Can you teach me to throw, I said not today, I got a lot to do, he said, that's okay." The opportunity for the *SJ* is to leverage every bit of the value of being the dependable doer of the activities of each day while learning to set aside the list when those more important moments come our way which are not on the list.

I believe Mary was an *NP*. *Ns* are good at seeing the big picture and recognizing the significance of things in the world as they occur. They connect those events to the possibilities they present for something special. When you add the *Perceiving*, it equips the *NP* to always look for those break-through possibilities in life. They are not checking things off lists. They are adding novel items to the list which may push lesser important items aside.

Mary looks good in this story because Jesus reinforces her for seeing the importance of taking advantage of every moment with him. In another account of this story in John 12, we see Mary also recognized the true value of material things when she washed Jesus' feet with an expensive perfume. *NPs* are great at seeing the possibilities in life and being open to new and better ways of seeing and acting in our world. Their challenge is recognizing there are practical things that must be done at times. This will prevent them from taking advantage of those who are willing to do the necessary activities of life. As an *NP*, I have been guilty of creating new things on the list of my spouse, friends, or colleagues, and it is unfair for me to overlook doing those things. I am not driven by checking everything off a list, but they are. If they are important to me, I need to help with their list.

We have examined the dynamics of the of the *SJ/SP/NP/NJ* pairs of preferences. Being aware of how these pairs of preferences impact our response to daily situations can be helpful in improving our effectiveness in those moments.

- **What:** The *SJ/SP/NP/NJ* pairs tell us a lot about how we function in diverse ways from each other at times.
- **So What:** By understanding the strengths and pitfalls of each pair, I can look for opportunities to leverage my strengths and those of others while also being more understanding of the potential pitfalls and how we can work together to minimize the adverse impact of those shortcomings.
- **Now What:** I will seek to value what we each bring to situations and be graceful toward myself and others for the things which are challenging for us.

CHAPTER 10

MBTI AND PROBLEM-SOLVING/ DECISION-MAKING

I n the next two chapters we will consider two critical areas of our lives. Problem-solving/decision-making and communications are two of the most critical capabilities needed to be effective in life. In this chapter, we will consider how good and bad decisions and ability or inability to solve difficult problems can impact our lives. We can all identify decisions which significantly impacted our lives for better or worse. It is not difficult to reflect on how the resolution of a problem life presented us worked out great and was nothing more than a bump in the road. We can also probably recall a problem we failed to resolve, and the result was a significant setback in our lives.

The preferences which have a major influence on the way we approach decisions and problems are the *Perceiving* preferences of *Sensing* and *Intuition* and the *Judging* preferences of *Thinking* and *Feeling*. These preferences are called the functions of MBTI because they deal with the way we perceive and address problems/decisions with the information available to us.

Isabel Briggs Myers (1980) believed we tend to use our preferred functions and neglect the others as we make decisions and solve problems. This could lead to consistently missing vital information that needs to be considered and not balancing logic and people impact in making the decision or solving the problem. Rather than trying to become good at the lesser preferred preferences, Myers believed we should do the following: "Whenever you have a problem to solve, a decision to make, or a situation to deal with, try exercising each process by itself--consciously and purposefully. That way each process can make its own contribution to the solution without interference from any other process. Start with your perceptive processes (*Sensing* and *Intuition*). Perception should always come before judgment."

Gordon Lawrence in *People Types and Tiger Stripes (1982) described this process as systematically walking through the S, N, T, and F functions in a zig-zag manner.* This is a wonderful model which uses the S/N/T/F functions to illustrate natural steps we go through in making decisions or responding to problems. Lawrence's model looks like this:

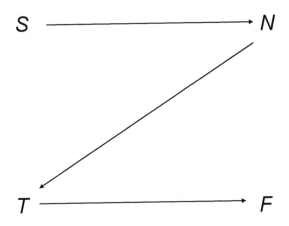

This model shows decision-making starting with a definition of the decision to be made or the problem to be solved. In making decisions we consider the following: what has happened; what facts are relevant to the problem or decision; what real world problem needs to be solved. This step deals with a real-world description of the problem/decision and all the facts, history, data, and information informing that problem/decision. This is where the *Sensing* preference is so important because this preference pays attention to the real world current and historical evidence gathered by the five senses. *Sensing* people are great at knowing the history and present facts about situations. This preference helps us know what "is."

The first thing *Sensing* helps us do is define exactly what the decision/problem is. Dorothea Brande, American writer and editor once said: "A problem clearly stated is a problem half solved." We need to have a clear understanding of the issues and be able to communicate them effectively to others so we can ensure we all are on the same page and working on the same issue and toward the same end.

Secondly, the *Sensing* preference helps us gather the information which will inform us and guide us as we try to make the best possible decision or effectively resolve the problem. We want to be thorough enough in the *Sensing* step to gather all helpful information and no more. People who have a dominant *Sensing* can get caught up in gathering excessive data because they love those details. They must learn to ask what information is really needed. People who are very clearly *Intuition* can get bored and impatient quickly with this step and start wanting to move on to possibilities. They need to learn to be disciplined enough to work with the *Sensing* people to gather the information needed.

Once we have completed the *Sensing* step and have defined the problem/decision clearly and have the information relevant to the problem/decision, we move to the *Intuition* step. This is where we begin identifying alternative ways to solve the problem or alternative options in relation to the decision. This is the brainstorming stage where we do not critique ideas, but we generate possibilities. Having completed the *Sensing* step, the brainstorming should be focused on the problem/decision we have defined and not something else. In addition, having looked at the practical realities related to the problem/decision, we should be generating innovative ideas that are not obviously outside the realm of possibilities. Brainstorming will be informed by reality.

This step is where people with a preference for *Intuition* thrive. People who prefer *Intuition* love using their hunches and imagination about possibilities. This is where the *Sensing* people need to keep an open mind. It is tempting for them to reject an idea because it does not currently exist in a tangible form. It is important for them to ask themselves the question, "how could we make this idea work?" This is where the synergy between *Intuition* and *Sensing* can generate innovative possibilities. Those with *Intuition* will throw out a "wild and crazy" idea and the *Sensing* can then begin to consider how to make the idea work in a practical way. This type of collaboration can produce creative approaches to addressing problems/decisions which may seem overwhelming initially.

After we have completed the N step, we should have identified 2-5 alternative solutions to the problem or 2-5 choices for the decision. This brings us to the *T* step where we use *Thinking* to analyze the solutions/choices we have identified. The *T* step provides the opportunity to dive into the logical analysis of our alternatives. This involves a consideration of the pros and cons of each alternative. This is where we consider the facts and data, we gathered in the S step, and options generated in the N step.

The *Thinking* step is critical to helping us make sure we do not make a stupid decision by not considering the relevant factors related to this problem/decision. Our *Thinking* people will love this step because they enjoy analyzing advantages and disadvantages of solutions/choices, and they will bring a brutal honesty to the evaluation. This will enable us to eliminate poor options and be guided toward more reasonable choices/solutions. This analysis will often involve weighing the most crucial factors to be considered and will usually lead us to a ranking of the solutions/choices from top to bottom.

The potential pitfalls to be aware of during this *T* step includes what we have all experienced at times, and it is called "paralysis from analysis." This means we might analyze things beyond what is necessary. Every problem and decision in life needs a reasonable degree of analysis, and the degree will vary depending on the situation. At some point, analysis becomes counter-productive, because it does not add additional value to the solution/choice.

Another pitfall is when those who are *Feeling* do not engage in the step. Those who are *Feeling* will have the tendency to want to primarily focus on the impact of the solution/choice on people. We will get to this consideration in the *F* step, but it is important for those with a preference for *Feeling* to engage in the *T* step to consider the logic as it relates to exploring the impact on people.

The *F* step is the last one in the problem-solving/decision-making process. We start this step with a list of alternative solutions/choices generated in the *N* step that has been placed in a ranked order based on the logical analysis conducted in the *T* step for the problem/decision we defined and explored in the *S* step. In the *Feeling* step we are going to consider how the alternative solutions/choices impact the people involved.

People with a preference for *Feeling* bring empathy into the equation. They have the gift of putting themselves into the shoes of others and understanding, to the best of their ability, how things affect others. *Fs* will work diligently in this step to consider how each solution/choice is most likely to impact the people involved. The *Fs* will advocate for solutions/choices of greatest benefit for those affected and will speak against the solutions/choices which would do harm to the people involved. *Fs* must remember they are speaking to the *Ts* who primarily approach solutions/choices logically. It is not because they do not care about the people affected. They just view the people impact as one more piece of data that needs to be weighed. They might recognize the importance of giving consideration to the people impact, but it will often have to be brought to their attention. This is where the *Fs* needs to respect the *Ts* rational approach and present factors related to people impact in a way the *T* can see and weigh in his/her logical analysis.

We are confronted every day with important decisions, and we frequently encounter problems which need to be resolved. We are using parts of the *S/N/T/F* process over and over every day in some manner. Being able to devote appropriate attention to each step in the process is important. As an *ENFP*, I love investing time in the *N* step and generating many innovative ideas which "might" work. I am also strongly invested in the *F* step and devote a lot of attention to how people are impacted. However, years ago I realized neglecting the *S* and *T* steps could create major problems. The most dramatic example of this for me was in buying cars. I would love to have the money I have wasted on bad car purchases. These bad decisions resulted from not gathering the critical data about factors like reliability, service costs, and resale value. I sure identified a lot of great possibilities, but they were not generated after considering some very practical information related to my decision. In addition, I did not weigh the pros and cons of the alternatives in a sound logical manner. I jumped too quickly to the *F* step, and I would then choose the car that I liked best. Neglecting the *S* and *T* steps resulted in buying cars like the little red sports car which became a huge money pit due to numerous repairs.

After finally recognizing the error of my ways, I became much better at gathering good data from sources like J.D. Power ratings and my mechanic. I also developed a decision matrix to analyze the key factors in buying the best car for my needs. This analysis resulted in me identifying my top two choices from a *T* viewpoint, and then I use my *F* and buy the one I liked most. This process has led to much better purchases of automobiles.

- **What:** *Sensing, Intuition, Thinking,* and *Feeling* relate to important steps in any problem-solving/ decision-making process. Some situations may dictate one or more steps require additional attention. For example, when you are making decisions related to the death of a loved one, logic is much less important than how the loved ones are affected.

- **So What:** Making sure I pay attention to each step of the S/N/T/F process is important in making good decisions and solving problems.
- **Now What:** I will respect and value the perspective each step brings and ensure I devote appropriate attention to each step even though it might not be natural for me. At times, I might need to get assistance in completing certain steps because it is a challenge for me to utilize a preference in the manner needed to make the best decision or solve the problem.

CHAPTER 11

MBTI AND COMMUNICATIONS

I love the countless resources on MBTI which help you understand and apply the concepts. There is so much more material available about MBTI than any other personality assessment. I have observed people become quite expert in applying MBTI concepts through self-study. Sometime simple guides like *Introduction to Type and Communications* by Donna A. Dunning (2003) can be so helpful in utilizing MBTI to improve our communication skills.

Communications is one of the most important abilities for living a successful life and having meaningful and effective relationships. In counseling with hundreds of couples over the years, a breakdown in communications was the major factor in bad marriages, and effective communications was a key to successful marriages. In the workplace, I have observed employees who were experts in their field and had a fervent desire to succeed have an unsuccessful career due to their poor communications skills. I have seen a good understanding and application of MBTI transform poor marriages into good marriages and ineffective employees into high performers.

I would like to share some ways I have observed MBTI helping in this major area of communications. One of the best ways of using MBTI to improve communications is to simply consider the way individual preferences affect communications. In counseling with couples or someone struggling with communications, I might ask them to review the material from *Introduction to Type and Communications* and see how they could be more attentive to their spouse's communications needs. The following are some simple hints for improving communications:

- If I am an *E* and the other person is an *I*, it is important to share my concerns with that person and allow them to think about it before they respond.
- If I am an *I* and the other person is an *E*, it is important to allow them to "think out loud" and talk things out after I have had the opportunity to get my thoughts in order.
- If I am an *S* and the other person is an *N*, I need to understand they are not focusing on details but on the big picture and how things fit together,
- If I am an *N* and the other person is an *S*, I need to have an appreciation for how important the details of a situation are to them.
- If I am an *T* and the other person is an *F*, I need to recognize the importance of value considerations and the personal impact on people as we discuss decisions.
- If I am an *F* and the other person is a *T*, I need to understand the importance of determining whether it is logical to pursue a certain path. *T*s can best be influenced with data and analysis.
- If I am a *J* and the other person is a *P*, I need to appreciate their need for flexibility and the ability to adapt and move in a different direction if needed.
- If I am a *P* and the other person is a *J*, I need to value their need to reach closure and have a clear sense of what the plan and path forward is.

Many years ago, I worked for someone who was a clear *ISTJ*, and I am clearly an *ENFP*. We were the opposite on every preference and these differences often reared their ugly head. We had a lot of respect for each other and had a genuine desire to work together to accomplish things we both had a strong commitment to achieving. However, we frequently butted heads along the road to getting there. He once told me I was the most stubborn person he had ever supervised, and I told him I had heard that before. I shared with him I inherited that gene from my mother. But after one of our argumentative meetings, I realized a major part of our problem was due to our MBTI differences.

When I came in for our next meeting, I brought tent cards with an *ISTJ* for him and an *ENFP* for me. I put his in front of him and placed mine in front of me. Since he was familiar with MBTI, I shared with him that in the future I was going to be more considerate of his preferences when I communicated with him. In consideration of his preferences, I would: provide him time to reflect; share information about the facts around the issue we were discussing; present a logical analysis of alternative proposals; and provide a detailed plan of our path forward. I also asked him to consider my preferences and how they were important in the role I was playing in the organization. We had a great discussion, and our relationship became much more effective and enjoyable after we made some changes in the way we communicated and worked together.

About a year ago, a manager in Company B contacted me and indicated she had two employees who played a similar role in a training and development group she led, and they needed to work together as a team and were struggling to do so. She indicated they were both great people and very capable but were having difficulty working together. It was critical for them to cooperate with each other to manage the flow of work related to their roles. After discussing the problems, we decided to have a half-day workshop where we would examine their working relationship through the lens of MBTI.

Through the years, I have found MBTI to be a great tool for exploring relationship issues in a very non-threatening way. It is not about: who is right or wrong; who is good or bad; or, skilled or unskilled. It works from an understanding we all have a basic natural set of personality preferences. They are often different, and that is OK. This is the reason we thought MBTI would provide a way to look at their relationship in a positive and constructive manner.

When they came for the workshop, each employee had a great attitude. When I asked them what they wanted to accomplish, they agreed they wanted to work together in a manner which would produce high quality results for their area of responsibility and in a way that would be fun and rewarding for them. This matched the objectives their manager had for the workshop. We followed the following process to hopefully achieve those results.

- Review their MBTI types with an understanding they were different on three of the four preferences.
- Look at the differences in their preferences and pairs of preferences and discuss how they see those differences contributing to their difficulties in working together.
- Develop a plan of what each of them will do differently to improve the effectiveness of the relationship and what they will do jointly to enhance their work results and enjoyment in working together.

As I mentioned they were different on three of the four preferences. Co-worker One was an *ISTJ* and co-worker Two was an *ENFJ*. In *Introduction to Type and Teams*, a snapshot of each of the sixteen types is provided. The snapshots of One's *ISTJ* and Two's *ENFJ* are:

- *ISTJ*: Thorough, hardworking, and responsible, *ISTJs* work well within traditional structures, following standard procedures and keeping track of facts and details. They clarify responsibilities and roles, seek to maintain what is efficient and useful, and follow through on their commitments. **Major Characteristic: Dependability.**

- *ENFJ*: Warm, supportive, and friendly, *ENFJs* work well when they can focus on people's aspirations, develop organized plans to meet goals, and maintain integrity as they work. They tune into others—easily getting to know their hopes and dreams—foster collaborations and strive for the common good. **Major Characteristic: Affiliation**

As you can see, these coworkers are quite different. When we began working on ways to enable them to work together in a highly effective manner, they identified the following improvement plan:

Coworker One (*ISTJ*) identified these actions he would take to improve their working relationship:

- Express interest in ideas or issues and intent to give it more consideration and make a commitment to get back to the other person within a specific time frame.
- Hear coworker Two out and make sure I understand how issues will impact people.

Coworker Two (*ENFJ*) identified these actions he would take to improve their working relationship:

- Give Coworker One time to think about things before pushing for a response and ensure Coworker One has shared the relevant facts in situations and the logic behind his perspective.
- Give more consideration to thoughts I throw out before expressing them.

Joint actions they will both take to improve working relationship:

- Consider *S/N* difference in assigning projects such that Coworker One has more long-term and detailed projects while Coworker Two has more of the quicker turn around projects.
- Better communicate basis of decisions due to *T/F* differences.
- Channel all project requests through joint discussion and decision process for assigning the project.
- Have huddle time each day if needed to make project assignment decisions.
- In making project decisions, balance One's practical perspective and Two's tendency to take on too much. This would result in stretching a little at times while insuring they both do not take on more than they can do in a quality manner.

All employees in Company B receive MBTI training, and as we will discuss in the Leadership/ Personal Development chapter, Company B utilizes MBTI extensively in the areas of coaching and team development. In addition, Company B will occasionally do workshops with a specific learning objective and use MBTI concepts to assist in achieving that objective.

Company B has an annual Management Council Workshop at the end of the year where they look back at the performance of the organization for the previous year and forward toward the goals and plans for the coming year. A few years ago, the CEO wanted to have a learning activity on communications and asked me to help. The workshop followed the following process:

Divided the ninety participants into eight groups of *STs, SFs, NFs,* and *NTs.* These small groups discussed the following:

- What are key factors of good communications?

- How do you facilitate good communications on a team?
- Select someone to record your responses on a clip board and share with the large group.

As each group reported back the results of their discussion, we examined how their preferences on the MBTI functions influenced the way they communicate. These are things which came out of that discussion:

STs:

- Paraphrasing what you hear can help assure others we understand each other.
- Recognize we will not always agree and that is OK.
- Focus on facts and manage emotions.
- Be specific and direct while respectful.

SFs:

- Seek agreement and harmony.
- Respecting others is essential.
- Listen attentively to the thoughts and feelings of others.
- Communicate without anger and pay attention to the feelings of others.

NFs:

- Respecting others is foundational.
- Seek to work toward a common vision.
- Seek to understand the other person.
- We look for agreement in a collaborative way.
- Express thoughts and feelings in a caring way.

NTs:

- Maintain strong focus on what we are trying to accomplish and do not bring unnecessary information into the discussion.
- Ensure there is a fair exchange of information: content and process as well as the verbal and nonverbal cues need to be considered.
- Do not beat around the bush. Communicate directly and to the point while being respectful.

Processing the above information led to the following conclusions. By understanding how different preferences define effective communication, it is possible to identify how we can bridge the gaps between varied assumptions about the best methods for communicating. All the preferred styles of communication have value and diversity which, if appreciated and embraced, can improve the quality of our communications and the outcomes associated with those interactions.

The CEO made the following observation about the value of the communications workshop in a note to the Management Council: "The Myers-Briggs workshop served to reinforce (among other things) how caring, respect, and honesty play into communications as well as the value of repetition and keeping things simple/understandable."

Effective communication is essential for understanding. Others will not understand me unless I can communicate in a manner which enhances their ability to understand. Also, I will not understand others unless I first understand the way in which they communicate. MBTI provides a powerful framework for improving communications and thus understanding.

- **What:** Each of our natural personality preferences affect the way we communicate and a difference in preferences can present challenges in communicating effectively.

- **So What:** By understanding the influence of MBTI preferences on the way we communicate, we can communicate in a manner which will better meet each of our needs.
- **Now What:** By being intentional in considering the MBTI preferences of other people and my own, I can tailor my communications to facilitate mutual understanding.

CHAPTER 12

MBTI AND CAREER CHOICE

Around 2005, my wife and I were teaching the high school youth at our church, and they wanted to discuss career choices. I shared with them about the Myers-Briggs Type Indicator® Career Report, and how and we could generate a report for each of them to help them explore career interests. They were excited about doing it, so I ordered the assessments. After I distributed the assessments to the young people, I had an additional one, and I asked my wife, Marcie, if she would like to complete an assessment. She was approaching her 20th year as an Office Manager for a physician's medical practice, and she thought it would be fun to do the assessment. A couple of weeks later, I received the Career Reports and began looking over them in preparation for sharing them with the young people. As I reviewed Marcie's results, I became a little concerned when I saw the top career match for a person with her type. I took her results to her and asked her if she was happy. With a puzzled look, she responded with a yes. I then asked her if she was happy being married to me. She said, "of course I am" and wanted to know why I was asking. I told her I received her career report, and when I saw her top career match, I became a little concerned. I handed her the report and she looked at the report and began to laugh. The top match for her type was a nun in the Catholic order. My wife would have made a wonderful nun because she is so kind and compassionate, but I am glad she did not like everything associated with that role in life.

When we are making a career choice, we need to consider many things. The following is a model I have used with youth and adults in helping them to explore what career options might be best for them.

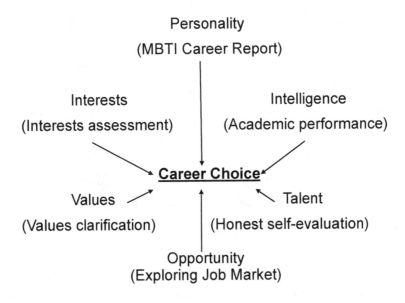

As you can see, many factors impact our career choice. It is important to consider my natural intelligence and the way I have developed that academically. We all knew the kids who excelled in various areas like math, English, and history. Yes, we can develop greater knowledge in areas but most of us were not naturally equipped to be rocket scientist.

We need to examine what talents we naturally have or could develop and what influence those talents might have on our career choice. As a youth, I could throw a football well and started as quarterback on my high school football team for two years. However, I did not have other physical gifts that would enable me to be the next Johnny Unitas (from my day). This is the observation my high school coach made about my foot speed: "Rick, your major problem is you run too long in one place." As a result, football became a spectator sport after high school.

It is important to examine our values to see how they match with certain career options. If I develop a major desire to serve and help people, then I might steer away from a technical career even though I am good in math. Values are a result of the way we are nurtured by family and the culture in which we are raised although our natural personality has some influence.

The interests we develop in our lives also have a major influence on our career choice. Interests are determined by a combination of nature and nurture. Our interests may develop in a variety of areas like business, technical, social issues, arts, sports, and crafts. There are effective interest assessments like the Strong Interest Inventory, which assesses you against general occupational themes like: realistic, investigative, artistic, social, enterprising, and conventional.

An exploration of career opportunities and whether I will be able to find a job in a specific career is a practical issue we need to consider.

The final area to consider in any career choice is how well does my personality match with the work involved in a specific career. This is where the Myers-Briggs Type Indicator® Career Report can be of tremendous assistance. This report can help you:

- Identify a broad family of jobs to begin exploring
- Identify strengths and potential weaknesses of your type for the career search process
- Plan your career development strategy and next steps
- Choose job path(s) that are the best fit for your personality
- Determine educational path
- Make a career transition or shift
- Enhance job satisfaction

The Myers-Briggs Type Indicator® Career Report has shed a great deal of light on my career path. I did not have the benefit of using it for my first career choice and that helps to explain why I spent only two years and nine months in that job.

I began my college career in engineering because I was good at math and engineering was a good career path in terms of opportunities and financial reward. I quickly realized even though I was making good grades, I hated engineering physics, calculus, and all the other technical courses. I decided I wanted to work with people and explored several majors and found there was a personnel management focus in the industrial management program which would prepare me to work in the field of human resources. My degree gave me a broad background in accounting, finance, economics, marketing, and general business, in addition to personnel management. I loved it and did well.

The job I chose after college was with Company A who had a great reputation and was considered a leader in Industrial Relations at that time. I was hired into the Wage Standards and Industrial Engineering Department. My responsibilities were helping the sales, marketing, and technical service areas of the company manage their performance management and pay systems.

I was miserable. It was a great company. I worked with great people, and the work we did was important. However, it was not a good fit for me. The role I had involved establishing standards and procedures for compensation and evaluation of employee performance and insuring we operated consistently in compliance with those procedures and any laws related to compensation and evaluations of employees.

I later discovered this work was a perfect match for *ISTJs*, and many of the employees doing this work had types close to an *ISTJ*. My MBTI type is *ENFP*. Do you see the problem? My type was exactly the opposite of the type for people who were a good match for this work.

I was beginning to explore other career options when a felt a spiritual calling to go into the ministry. As a result, I left Company A under good circumstances and went to seminary to become a minister. While in seminary I began ten years of serving in the ministry in church and college settings. During the last three years of that period, I completed the course work for a doctorate in Educational and Counseling Psychology with the intent of becoming a counselor. When I was about to finish my course work, I received a call from Company A wanting to know if I was interested in interviewing for a position as Coordinator of an Employee Assistance Program which they were starting. This program would provide free counseling and referral assistance to employees and family members for any type of personal, psychological or substance abuse problem. After pledging I would never go back to work for Company A, they made me an offer I could not refuse, and I returned to begin ten years of starting and managing the Employee Assistance Program which helped thousands of employees and family members.

At the end of those ten years, I moved into the training department to work with my friend Zellie in the areas of personal, team, leadership, and organizational development. I have continued to do that type of work for fifteen years at company A and for the last fifteen years since retiring from Company A.

My work experiences for almost 50 years since leaving Company A early in my career have been in the top five most attractive job families for *ENFPs*. I can say during all those years, my job has not been "work" for me. I have loved the work associated with every job I have had. At 75 years of age, people ask me when I am going to retire, and I do not have an answer. My work is more about who I am than just what I do.

This is what a Myers-Briggs Type Indicator® Career Report is supposed to help you discover. It can help you find those careers where your personality can flourish and find expression. In addition, it will contribute to helping you find that job which will not only be a joy for you but help you make contributions to those who employee you, work with you, and are served by you.

- **What:** People perform best and with the greatest satisfaction when their personality is a good match with the work they do.
- **So What:** MBTI can help me examine how my personality matches with job families and specific jobs.
- **Now What:** If we are unhappy in our job or a young person is trying to make a career choice, we can seek someone who is certified to use MBTI and complete a Myers-Briggs Type Indicator® Career Report to assist in our career choice.

CHAPTER 13

MBTI AND PERSONAL/ LEADERSHIP DEVELOPMENT

For the last 30 years, I have used MBTI extensively in organizational settings with a primary focus on personal, leadership, and team development. In the next chapter we will focus on team development, and in this chapter, we will examine how individuals can use MBTI to provide an understanding of themselves and others in a way to become more effective individually and as leaders.

The work I've been so fortunate to do utilizing MBTI includes the following:

- With Company A, conducted MBTI workshops with over 1,000 employees.
- With Company B, taught MBTI to over five hundred employees.
- MBTI workshops with over 1,000 leaders in area community leadership programs.
- Taught applications of MBTI to leadership for about three hundred managers and potential managers with Company B.
- Used MBTI extensively with a small company as a part of providing

organizational development support.

- Led MBTI workshops in 15 different countries in Europe, Asia, North and South America.
- Utilized MBTI with other companies and non-profits as a part of consulting engagements.

Over fifty million people have taken the MBTI in 115 countries, and eighty-eight of the Fortune 100 companies have utilized the MBTI within the last 5 years. No other instrument of its type comes close to this level of usage.

I share these numbers to show you the value of MBTI over time. I have seen it used to help develop employees and teams in three successful organizations over three decades. It was helpful in developing community leaders who could become more effective in leading community efforts over a period of twenty plus years. Over the last 14 years, Company B has used MBTI to develop a language for understanding themselves and others in order to improve the way they work together and serve members.

Every MBTI workshop I lead ends with a personal exercise providing participants with the opportunity to apply what they have learned in a practical way to improve their personal effectiveness. The concepts of MBTI provide a wonderful non-threatening way to look at ourselves honestly and identify our strengths and what we do well naturally. In addition, we can identify the things which get in our way at times and prevent us from getting the results we want. The beauty about MBTI is it puts us all on the same level playing field. We all have strengths, and we all have weaknesses. MBTI helps us understand those strengths and weaknesses. It also enables us to affirm what we do well and laugh about the things which get us in trouble. MBTI helps us acknowledge without hesitancy the things we do well and express without shame the areas in which we struggle. When most people learn what their four preferences mean and how they influence their behavior, they usually smile and say, "That's me."

Nathaniel Branden said: "The first step toward change is awareness. The second step is acceptance." As a minister, counselor, teacher and consultant, my work with people has been about change. I was working with people who were seeking to: grow emotionally, spiritually, and in relationships; achieve career success; or improve organizational performance. MBTI was one of the most effective tools in my toolkit to help create awareness and acceptance of the need to change.

Anyone who has at least two children knows we are all different and we bring different strengths and shortcomings with us into this world. These natural differences in preferential tendencies move us toward effectiveness in certain areas and lack of effectiveness in others. Once we have that awareness, we are in an outstanding position to make desired change.

I was blessed to have good professors in my doctoral program who gave me great guidance in how to use assessment instruments appropriately with people. The training and certification process by the Center for the Application of Psychological Type was also beneficial. The opportunity to collaborate with my friend, Zellie, over a period of about ten years in applying MBTI to many learning issues and performance problems taught me so much. These influences led me to focus workshops on helping people understand the preferences, combination of preferences and their type and how those influence our behavior. When people gain awareness and acceptance of their basic personality, it often enables them to bring about positive change. However, I also believed being intentional about translating that awareness into action would accelerate real change.

The MBTI introductory workshops would close with the following exercise. It involved them answering the following questions and then sharing their responses with the class:

Review the material for your preferences and your four-letter type and answer the following questions:

- What are your major strengths based on your preferences and type, and how can you best utilize and leverage them to improve your effectiveness?
- What challenges do you face based on your preferences and type, and what actions can you take to prevent them from adversely impacting your effectiveness?

Helping explore opportunities to better utilize their strengths and maximize the value from those behaviors was the first focus. The goal was to encourage people to play to their strengths and put themselves in positions where their behavior is natural and not forced. I am always most effective in situations where adapting is more critical than organization. I have been fortunate to build my life around those strengths.

The consideration of the second question about how we address the challenges associated with our preferences and type is important also. As we gain an understanding of why we struggle in certain areas of our lives, we can find ways to compensate or improve enough in that area to prevent the weakness from adversely affecting us. Let us examine a couple of examples.

For a period of about ten years, I traveled a good bit internationally. On those trips, I would usually visit various locations in an area like Europe. I would often be teaching classes in those locations which required materials to be there for participants. The travel plans and shipping of materials was a logistical nightmare especially for an *ENFP*. Planning details around a schedule is a weakness of my type. Fortunately, I had two work associates who were *SJs*. One was our administrative assistant, and the other was a travel planner for the company. When the locations, dates, and courses for the trip were defined, I would get with these two colleagues, and they took care of everything. The travel planner would hand me my itinerary and tickets, and my administrative assistant would assure me the materials would be in the appropriate places, and they always were. I never checked these two *SJs* because it would have been a waste of my time. They were playing to their strengths and helping me compensate for my weakness. This is not taking advantage of another person. I have often worked with people where it was a complementary relationship. I would do things which they did not do well and did not want to do and vice versa. These were mutually valued relationships.

At times we cannot find a mutually beneficial relationship to help us compensate for a weakness. This is where we need to develop processes to help strengthen our weaknesses. For example, since the two *SJ* colleagues I mentioned earlier were only available at work, I have had to learn some time management tools and planning tools to help me manage appointments and responsibilities in my personal life. By using these tools which are not too elaborate or detailed I am able to be where I need to be and do the things I need to do in a responsible manner. These tools would not be as detailed and structured as an *SJ* would prefer, but they work fine for this *NP*. These tools keep me sufficiently on track. They enable me to use my major strengths of adapting when things occasionally get off track.

One of the most rewarding things about teaching MBTI over the years has been having people who attended workshops come up and share stories about how they had been able to make positive intentional changes. Often these minor changes significantly improved the quality of their lives. This is what the power of understanding can produce in our lives and MBTI can really enhance our understanding of ourselves.

Company B has an ongoing coaching and development process for all employees. Each employee develops a plan for what they will do in the coming year to become more effective. It could be leveraging a strength, improving in an area, developing a new skill, or gaining some relevant knowledge. They develop this plan and review it with their manager. They then receive coaching in relation to that plan.

Since all employees in Company B have training in MBTI and managers receive additional training on how to use MBTI in coaching employees, Company B provides an MBTI Personal Development Guide in the Managers' Toolkit online site. This is a tool managers can use to help employees identify development goals using the MBTI lens. I am including this guide as a resource for managers who struggle to define development objectives for employees. It is also useful for individuals to use in their own personal growth journey.

This guide requires a resource which Company B makes available to employees. That tool is the booklet, *Introduction to Type in Organizations*. This booklet can be purchased on Amazon. Hopefully, you will find this personally helpful or useful in an organizational setting.

MBTI Personal Development Guide

A key factor in being a good leader is developing your talent so they can perform at a high level and contribute positively to organizational performance. This development aspect of your coaching/ leadership role involves: getting people in the position that best fits their capabilities; leveraging the strengths of the people you lead; and helping employees improve or compensate in areas where development is needed.

Management works with Human Resources to get people in the "right seat on the bus." Providing feedback to employees about their strengths and finding ways to use them is not difficult. However, having development discussions is not always an easy thing because pointing out mistakes, failures, or weaknesses can be uncomfortable and a challenge to confront.

The Myers-Briggs Type Indicator, which measures our natural behavioral preferences, provides a constructive framework and tool for development discussions. The Coaching and Development Process is excellent and should always be used as the overarching process. The following steps can be used in this process at times to facilitate a constructive coaching session:

1. Ensure the people you supervise have taken the MBTI and completed an MBTI workshop. Find the page for the employee's type in the *Introduction to Type in Organizations* booklet. Review the information about the employee's type and determine how the employee's natural behavioral preferences are influencing their job performance. Highlight those areas and prepare to review those with the employee.

2. As a part of the employee's coaching and development discussion, explain how our natural behavioral preferences have a significant impact on the way we approach our job duties, and as a result you want to review strengths and opportunities for development using MBTI type as a guide. Refer to the page for the employee's type in the *Introduction to Type in Organizations* booklet and the following steps to guide that discussion:

   a. Leveraging employee strengths:
      1. Contributions to the Organization: Discuss items under this section which apply to them and any other contributions to positively reinforce the employees' strengths and how they contribute to the organization's success.
      2. Leadership Style: Discuss ways they demonstrate leadership in their team and ways they can utilize their leadership ability to help the team.
      3. Preferred Learning Style: Discuss ways they can utilize their learning style to continue to grow.
      4. Problem-Solving Approach: Review ways they can utilize their problem-solving strengths to help the team improve.
      5. Preferred Work Environments: Discuss ways to create the best working environment for them.

   b. Addressing development areas for improvement:

1. Problem-Solving Approach: Explore things the employee can do to improve their problem-solving ability.

2. Preferred Work Environments: Determine ways to adapt to the work environment if it does not fit their preferences.

3. Potential Pitfalls and Suggestions for Development: Review the potential pitfalls for this MBTI type and determine if these create problems for this employee at times. If any do, examine the suggestions for development to determine if there are things the employee can do to improve.

c. Take the top one to three ideas related to leveraging strengths and addressing areas for development from the discussion and document those in the coaching and development plan.

The focus so far in this chapter has been personal development. My primary use of MBTI over the years has been in workshops with leadership teams and in leadership training. The stories I have shared are based on the way I have observed MBTI influencing the decisions and behaviors of leaders. I have observed leaders become expert in their understanding of MBTI and applying it to leading people. The following is what a member of Company B's senior leadership team shared with me about his appreciation for and application of MBTI.

"MBTI as a part of leadership training helped create awareness for me that there are "different tools in the toolbox." On a leadership retreat during a problem-solving exercise, some of us stood back to size up the challenge; others plowed ahead quickly, eager to solve the challenge before the other teams finished. As I have managed people over the years, it has been helpful to understand dominant traits of people and try to help them lead with those traits in a part of our business where they can be successful and enjoy what they are doing."

In the leadership training at Company B, MBTI applications in the areas of coaching, team development, and communications are a part of each of the two 4-day leadership courses. Below are questions we discuss in each of the leadership courses to help leaders explore and utilize MBTI concepts in practical way.

Applications in first leadership course

Coaching:

- For your assigned MBTI preference, address the following:
  - What ways can each of the preferences contribute positively to the success of Company B?
  - What problems can each of the preferences create for Company B?
- For the assigned MBTI four-letter type:
  - Develop a coaching plan utilizing their potential strengths and minimizing the impact of their potential weaknesses.
- For your MBTI four letter-type:
  - Develop a coaching plan utilizing your potential strengths and minimizing the impact of your potential weaknesses.

Team Development: Based on the MBTI profile of this team:

- What are the natural strengths of this team?
- What are the potential shortcomings of this team?
- What could you do as a leader to improve the effectiveness of this team?

Application in second leadership course

Communications:

Based on your type, how can you as a leader improve the way you communicate with the people you lead and other leaders within ECU? In the book, *Good to Great*, Jim Collins identified characteristics which enabled companies to break out of the pack and move from good to great. The first characteristic he points out is what he called Level 5 Leadership. He observed the great companies had leaders who exhibited the paradoxical qualities of being a humble leader while having intense determination and professional will. Through the years I have been able to observe many Levels 5 leaders who were driven while at the same time being humble enough to know how important the people around them were. Many of these leaders utilized MBTI very effectively to understand the different things people bring to the table. These leaders recognized their perspective was never complete, and by understanding themselves and others, they could draw on others for ideas, viewpoints, and strengths which always improves the outcome for everyone. MBTI is a great tool to facilitate that type of understanding.

- **What:** My growth as an individual or leader depends on my ability to recognize my strengths and weaknesses.
- **So What:** MBTI can assist me in a non-threatening way to understand what I naturally do well and what I may struggle with at times.
- **Now What:** I can be intentional in taking actions which will enable me to play to my strengths and compensate for my weaknesses.

CHAPTER 14

MBTI AND TEAMBUILDING

Around 1990, Company A, like other companies, recognized the need to create a more empowered team-based culture. Technology, the knowledge economy, and the pace of change were making the old hierarchical chain of command structure inadequate for a more complex and rapidly changing world.

In Company A, there were several senior leaders who were championing that movement, and my friend, Zellie, was the primary internal educator/ facilitator they looked to for assistance in making this significant cultural change. The role of the first line supervisor was changing from someone who told people what to do to a coach. As coaches their focus would be on developing the capability of people such that they knew what to do. The goal was to prepare employees to make more decisions and take more independent actions consistent with their role on the team.

A few years into that effort, I joined Zellie in providing training and experiential education to help employees and leaders to make that cultural shift. The officers of the company had a major retreat every two years and those retreats included complex experiential learning exercises designed to help them experience situations which simulated the need for teamwork. There were AHAs that occurred as they saw themselves shift into "'demand and control" mode which was the norm at that time. These behaviors invariably created problems in achieving what they were trying to accomplish. They began to see what changes they had to make to lead in an empowered and team-based culture. It was not an easy transition. They began to realize to effectively lead a group of people you had to understand we are all different in terms of what we contribute, and we are all motivated differently.

While writing this, I have been watching the documentary, *The Last Dance*, about Michael Jordan and the Chicago Bulls' 1997–98 season. It shares the story about them winning their sixth NBA championship in eight years and all the challenges they had to overcome. They were coached by Phil Jackson, who won eleven NBA championships which is more than any other coach in NBA history. One of the major qualities of Phil Jackson which distinguished him from other coaches was his ability to bring out the best in each player, even though they were extremely different. You could not find four people who were more different than Michael Jordan, Steve Kerr, Scottie Pippen, and Dennis Rodman. However, Phil Jackson had the ability to know what each of them needed to maximize their contribution to the team.

We needed to develop that ability in the leaders of Company A. The experiential exercises surfaced the need for a more empowering and coaching approach for leadership. This approach to leadership places a premium on building relationships with the people you lead. In building those relationships, it is critical to understand the way your personality interacts with the personality of the people you lead. As we have seen with the preferences, understanding similarities and differences has a major impact on communications, decision-making, and the way we work together.

With an emphasis on teamwork, it not only created a need for managers to better understand their employees and how they relate to them.

It also created a need for employees to understand how they relate to each other, their manager, and the groups or people with whom they interface.

To give you an illustration of how important these working relationships are, I want to share a situation Zellie, and I encountered in working with the European sales force of Company A. They had a major sales meeting every other year which all the employees attended. We had approximately 120 employees located in nine European sales offices. They were experiencing unhealthy competition between offices. The offices were competing with one another for the highest sales volume, and as a result, they were not sharing business opportunities and other valuable information between locations. Sales leadership believed this was adversely affecting total sales in the region.

Zellie and I designed an experiential exercise which simulated their business situation, and to successfully complete the exercise, you had to share information and resources between the ten teams we created for the exercise. The teams consisted of a mixture of people from various offices. At the beginning of the exercise, the teams competed and did not help each other. When it became obvious, they must cooperate, they began sharing information and resources and completed the exercise successfully.

In processing the things learned from this exercise, they began to see the problem competition between offices was creating. They realized cooperating between offices would increase sales in all the offices and the region. This was obviously in the best interests of the company and their self-interest. We identified behaviors and changes they could make which would create greater cooperation between offices and within the region.

One action we identified was providing MBTI training in all the sales offices and sharing results across the region. Zellie and I completed that training in all the sales offices during the following year. We followed-up with European sales leadership a year later. They indicated cooperation had improved significantly and sales in the region had grown at a much higher rate than anticipated. MBTI again had served as a great tool to increase understanding of self and others and was useful as a tool to promote better teamwork.

During the early 1990s, we used MBTI extensively in Company A with leadership teams to improve their teamwork and effectiveness. The following are comments by a department manager in Human Resources during that time, who later became the CEO of Company B, about his team's experience in using MBTI:

"When I was a manager on the HR division team at Company A, we had nine managers reporting to the Division head of HR. Everyone on the team, other than the medical director, recreation manager, and myself (payroll/HR systems manager) were industrial engineers. All ten of us did the MBTI and it turned out no one on the HR leadership team was *Feeling (F)*. We were all *T (Thinking)*. I was the only *Extravert* on the team. Our overall profile was an *ISTJ*, which is typical for an industrial engineer.

So here we were involved every day making decisions that impacted 12,000 employees, but none of us had the *"Feeling"* dimension of MBTI. This meant our team, when striving to make decisions, would not typically put a high priority on considering the impact of decisions on people. Several of us, for some time, had expressed concern we were making our decisions in a mechanical way. When the MBTI profile revealed no *Fs* on our team, even the industrial engineers agreed we needed to do something different to offset this team weakness.

We decided as a team that we would add a new agenda item as the last item every time we met as a team. The new agenda item involved a review and discussion of what potential impact any decision we made on that day had on employees. We also addressed that impact and communicated the impact to our employees.

This minor addition, in a brief period, began to help the HR team do a much better job of managing change. That one agenda item caused us to start doing a much better job of communicating changes to employees. We eventually began to clearly recognize that the positive changes we were making, when not explained effectively, could be viewed as negative changes by employees. Our communications in HR got much better and we began to get the same feedback across the company from both employees and management. We all learned life lessons about the importance and value of good open and honest communications in dealing with change of any kind. We also learned the value of having diversity of MBTI types across our company and within teams to do a better job with decision-making as well as communications."

I usually began every MBTI teambuilding workshop with the questions:

- What are the strengths of your team?
- What are the things you struggle with as a team?

We would then park those responses and come back to them as we looked at the MBTI profile for their team. It was amazing how the strengths they identified for their team matched the strengths associated with their MBTI team profile. Likewise, the weaknesses you would expect for a team with their MBTI team profile helped to explain the problems they were experiencing. This exercise created buy-in for making changes which would better leverage their strengths and minimize the areas with which they struggled.

In every workshop we did with leadership teams or a team of individual contributors, we sought to come away with concrete actions the team could take to improve their effectiveness and results as a team. We felt those actions plus the increased understanding of their preferences and the preferences of their team members would work together to drive improvement.

In Company B, we cover team development as a part of their first leadership course. We take a hypothetical team and walk through an exercise which explores the natural strengths and challenges this team would face and what might improve their effectiveness.

In Company B we also provide a MBTI Team Development Guide which is comparable to the MBTI Individual Development Guide discussed in the last chapter. This guide along with the *Introduction to Type in Organizations* booklet is a part of the first leadership course and provided as a tool to use with teams they lead. This guide is below:

MBTI Team Development Guide

The following is a guide for managers and their teams to use as a development tool. It will guide the manager and team members through a process to help identify natural team strengths and areas for potential improvement.

When the individual MBTI results are consolidated into a team profile, it reflects the dynamics of how the personalities of those team members interact to demonstrate a "team personality." This "team personality" will produce certain strengths which contribute to the success of the team and certain potential pitfalls which could reduce team effectiveness. By considering those strengths and potential pitfalls, a team can be intentional in planning ways to leverage and maximize strengths and minimize pitfalls.

Let us begin. Use the following steps to facilitate your team improvement process:

1. Ensure everyone on the team has taken the MBTI and completed an MBTI workshop.

2. Develop a team profile using the sample matrix below. Determine your "team type" by choosing the letter for each of the preferences (for example either E or I) which has the most team members with that preference. As an illustration, a sample team matrix for an ESFJ team is shown below.

3. Find page for your team type in *the Introduction to Type in Organizations* booklet. Discuss the following information about your team type and identify the following:

   a. What strengths do we have as a team that you can leverage to be even more effective?

   b. What areas do we have for improvement and what steps could the team take to be even more effective as a team?

   c. Have each team member review the page for their type and identify one strength they want to use to help the team and one area for improvement on which they will focus.

4. Consider the following suggestions based on the make-up of your team:

   a. *Extraversion* and *Introversion*:

      1. If your team is strongly extraverted, ensure that the introverts on the team are given the opportunity to provide their input.

      2. If you team is strongly introverted, use round-robin discussion to ensure everyone shares their ideas.

   b. *Sensing* and *Intuition*:

      1. If your team is strongly *Sensing*, be sure you spend time looking at new and diverse ways of doing things.

      2. If your team is strongly *Intuition*, be sure you address key details of the present situation and do not change unless it is an improvement in the way things are done.

   c. *Thinking* and *Feeling*:

1. If your team is strongly *Thinking*, ensure you have considered the impact of decisions and actions on employees and members.
2. If your team is strongly *Feeling*, ensure you address the pros and cons of tough decisions even though it might be difficult for the people involved.

   d. *Judging* and *Perceiving*:

   1. If your team is strongly *Judging*, be sure you are flexible in situations where change or delay is needed.
   2. If you team is strongly *Perceiving*, be sure you provide the structure required and act when needed

5. Select 1–3 actions from items 3 and 4 your team can take to be more effective as a team.

MBTI Sample Team Type Distribution

ISTJ	ISFJ	INFJ	INTJ
Mary Jim	Jane Pat		
ISTP	**ISFP**	**INFP**	**INTP**
	Ann		
ESTP	**ESFP**	**ENFP**	**ENTP**
	Betty (M)		
ESTJ	**ESFJ**	**ENFJ**	**ENTJ**
Cheryl	David Ellen Nancy	Rachel Sue	

Sample Preference Profile

	NO.	%		NO.	%
E	7	58%	I	5	42%
S	10	83%	N	2	17%
T	3	25%	F	9	75%
J	10	83%	P	2	17%

Sample Improvement Plan for an ESFJ Team:

1. Develop approach for surfacing differences and managing conflict.
2. Pay more attention to the logical and company-wide implications of their decisions and actions.
3. Seek input from outside the team about ways to improve.

The last example we will consider for using MBTI to develop teams is a special workshop. Most teams experience challenges at times, such as: changing the make-up of the team; additional responsibilities; and adapting to organizational changes. These changes often lead to a drop off in team performance or unresolved conflicts. Every team could benefit from just pausing and doing a check-step to see if there are potential areas for improvement.

I have done many of these MBTI workshops in various organizations from profits to non-profits, large and small, and diverse businesses including medical, education, industrial, financial, entertainment, and government. MBTI works across boundaries. The following is: a team profile for a function within Company B: the agenda for a workshop; and the targeted improvement outputs from that workshop.

Example of Team Workshop Profile
(Number of Each Type on the Team)

ISTJ	ISFJ	INFJ	INTJ
3	3	1	1
ISTP	**ISFP**	**INFP**	**INTP**
ESTP	**ESFP**	**ENFP**	**ENTP**
ESTJ	**ESFJ**	**ENFJ**	**ENTJ**
2	4	1	

Team Mix by Preference

	NO.	%		NO.	%
E	7	47%	I	8	53%
S	12	80%	N	3	20%
T	6	40%	F	9	60%
J	15	100%	P	0	0%

Agenda for the Workshop:

- Review MBTI profile
- Find page for your team type in the Introduction to Type in Organizations booklet. Review the information about your team type and identify the following:
  - What strengths do we have as a team that you can leverage to be even more effective?
  - What areas do we have for improvement and what steps could we take to be even more effective as a team?
  - Each team member will then review the page for their type and identify one strength they want to use to help the team and one area for improvement on which they will focus.
- Discuss what each of you identified for ways we can improve as a team and individually

Team Improvement Ideas from the Workshop:

1. Need to consider the bigger picture
2. Look for diverse ways to improve
3. Consider the pros and cons of everything
4. Be aware and considerate of different strengths of team members
5. Focus more on our purpose and why we are here
6. Listen to different ideas
7. Be more willing to go outside our comfort zone as it relates to what we do in our job or our team as whole
8. Make sure we do not neglect the logic in situations
9. Take more time to see when others need help
10. Be more flexible in relation to opinions and other ways of doing things
11. Speak out in a respectful way with ideas about ways to improve
12. Work on seeking and listening better to the ideas of others
13. Get your job right first and then look to help others
14. Pay attention to balancing fairness and special treatment
15. Help and ask for help

Hopefully, these examples of ways to use MBTI in teambuilding will help you see the value of MBTI in helping teams improve communications, conflict resolution, generating innovative solutions, and producing better results.

As a University of Tennessee graduate and major big Vol fan, I have tremendous respect for Pat Summitt, the legendary coach of the Lady Vols basketball team. Her accomplishments are unparalleled in college athletics. She won a silver medal in the Olympics as a player in 1976. She returned as the coach for the Olympic team in 1984 and led the U.S. to a gold medal. She was Naismith Basketball Coach of the Century in 2000. In thirty-eight seasons as coach at Tennessee, she had a record of 1,098 wins and 208 losses and her program maintained a

100 percent graduation rate for players who completed their eligibility at Tennessee. She had more wins than any other coach at the time of her retirement and won eight NCAA championships.

I remember seeing one of their games around 2010 when there were over 20,000 people in the stands. As a graduate student, 30 years earlier, I had seen them play before a few hundred people. I can remember thinking at that game in 2010 how amazing it was to see the incredible growth of interest in women's basketball over that length of time. Most people give Pat Summitt more credit than anyone else for building women's basketball into what it is today.

I share all of this about Pat Summitt, because if anyone understood teamwork, she did. Pat Summitt used MBTI with her teams. If it is good enough for Pat, it is good enough for me.

- **What:** Team effectiveness is significantly impacted by the manner in which we work together to accomplish something.
- **So What:** By understanding and learning to value the way my teammates approach situations, I can better utilize their talents and adapt my behavior to best help them and contribute what I do best to the team.
- **Now What:** By utilizing a framework for understanding the strengths and potential weaknesses associated with our various personalities, we can develop team processes to best utilize our talents to maximize team effectiveness.

CHAPTER 15

ORGANIZATIONAL DEVELOPMENT AND MBTI

My writing process for this book began with developing an outline and then doing a rapid-fire dump of ideas and stories I have accumulated over almost 50 years in using MBTI. After I finished the first draft, I completed edits and rewrites. The next step was sending it to family members and friends whose opinion I valued and asking for their feedback. This step was tremendously helpful and resulted in significant improvements.

One additional result of others reviewing my draft was creating this chapter entitled "MBTI and Organizational Effectiveness." The former CEO of Company B pointed out in his feedback how much MBTI contributed to the effectiveness of Company B and its ability to achieve a level of performance that placed them in the top 1-10 percent on the most significant and widely accepted metrics for the financial services industry. Working with Company B over the last 16 years on personal and leadership development and other areas of organizational development enabled me to observe them applying MBTI in a manner seldom demonstrated in most companies. MBTI was a critical piece of their leadership development as I described in the chapter on that topic.

Employees were also introduced to how they could use MBTI concepts to collaborate more effectively with coworkers and better serve their members. MBTI also provided a language which facilitated valuing differences and resolving conflict in very constructive ways. MBTI is used to help teams work more effectively together by improving communications and facilitating better decision-making. The following feedback from the CEO about the book describes the value he perceived MBTI providing in the organizational effectiveness of Company B:

"Your book could assist consultants immensely in helping a client visualize and see how MBTI can be utilized by a company or any organization to address and improve soft-side issues with which lots of organizations (even extremely successful ones) struggle.

What we did in Company B with the use of Myers-Briggs improved the organizational alignment, the integrity of our mission and vision, and our ability to communicate top to bottom and inside out as well as outside in. It also gave us an ability to understand differences in how individuals strive to solve problems which led to a better acceptance of "diversity of thought," which we came to understand as a real strength for us to get things done more efficiently and effectively. MBTI use also resulted in Company B staff being able to better accept all kinds of differences among each other. This acceptance of differences improved teamwork and problem-solving.

Company B Management and staff came to understand the power of putting differences to work for our company in a very practical and realistic way because they saw how well it worked to make everything better. It made personal relationship issues and big problems more approachable and manageable. MBTI facilitated Company B transitioning from a good organization to becoming a sustainable high performing organization widely recognized across our industry simply by the incredible annual results we achieved year after year. Our results were in the top 1 to 10 percent on any widely accepted metric that mattered in the financial services industry. MBTI had a lot to do with this transition to becoming a high-performing company."

For the last 30 years, a major part of my work life was in organizational development and effectiveness. This work involved teaching many leadership courses, working on team effectiveness, facilitating groups in strategic planning and resolution of various organizational issues, organizational design efforts, cultural transformations, and managing major organizational change. The stories about the applications of MBTI discussed in this book took place in the context of organizational development activities of this type. MBTI was invaluable in contributing to the success of those efforts.

The former CEO of Company B has described how we used MBTI in addressing a broad area of key organizational issues. In Company A, we used it extensively in teambuilding, leadership development and as a tool to address specific issues teams faced. Every employee did not take the MBTI as is the case in Company B. MBTI was used widely in Company A but not as strategically and extensively as Company B. I want to share two other organizational applications of MBTI before I suggest a strategy for using MBTI within an organization in such a manner that it can have a positive impact on organizational performance.

One organizational application of MBTI was unique. Zellie and I used the MBTI with a community leadership program. The community in which we lived had a population of about 70,000 people. Chambers of Commerce in most communities in the United States have community leadership programs. These programs select a group of individuals from the community each year with the mission of "developing leaders who give life to community dreams." They start the year off with a retreat and then meet one day each month for ten months with local leaders from government, business, healthcare, and education. They also take a trip to the state capital to meet with state legislators. They learn how positive change occurs in the community and develop networks which will enable them to be better agents of change. In addition, they break into small teams and work on a community improvement project which they present at the end of the ten months. Many positive changes in our community have come about due to these community projects.

The annual leadership program had been in existence for about ten years and my friend Zellie received a call from the director of the program saying she needed help. Zellie set up a meeting with three leaders of the program, himself, and me to discuss the situation. About thirty-two people from the community were in the program each year and it was critical for the group to get to know each other well and "bond" quickly because they had to hit the ground running so they could work well in their small teams to complete the community improvement projects. They had been struggling with developing those type of relationships for several years. Major problems had occurred the previous year during the opening retreat when they had some major conflicts between some participants. In one of the retreat exercises, participants got into arguments and a few hardly spoke to each other for the remainder of the ten months.

When we looked at the activities planned for the retreat, it was easy to understand the problems because they were using activities designed for use with a mature team which was seeking to develop significant conflict resolution skills. We recommended activities more appropriate for a large group of people coming together for the first time. These activities, which included teaching and applying MBTI, would help program participants get to know each other and learn to appreciate differences in a safe environment. We did the retreat that year and it was successful in meeting their objectives. For several years following, Zellie and I did the retreat together and after he moved on to some other things, I continued and led the retreat for twenty consecutive years. Over those years, we observed this new group of highly capable and motivated leaders come together quickly and form a highly cohesive group. They built trust and an appreciation of each other which helped them make significant contributions to the community. As word spread to other area leadership programs, this retreat format became the model for three other community leadership programs.

Each year the participants would complete an evaluation of the opening retreat and here are typical comments on what they liked most about the retreat:

- How to identify different personality types & work better as a group w/this information
- How we all have our place in the community & we need to work together to achieve the big picture
- Got to know team/class members easily—thought it would be hard to do; that not everybody thinks the same...figure out how to approach things to communicate better.
- Teamwork & cooperation among teams

We used MBTI to help participants get to know each other and their personalities. They learned to value each other's strengths and laugh about their differences. MBTI provided a non-threatening way to get to know and appreciate each other. We also used MBTI to put together the community improvement project teams. We wanted those teams to be diverse in terms of factors such as: male and female; different employers; different educational and work backgrounds; and, also, personality. As a result, we would make sure each team had all the preferences represented and a good mixture of each. The people who led the leadership program believed the quality of the projects improved by putting together diverse teams and providing them with tools to resolve any differences. MBTI helped them learn to value and utilize diverse perspectives.

The following are typical comments related to what they liked most about MBTI:

- My MBTI and how it affects my ability to work with others within the community.
- How easy different personalities can blend and accomplish a goal.
- I have done the Myers-Briggs on several retreats but the info about the diverse types was much better here. I feel I can use this info much better to understand myself and others and how to communicate with them.

This organizational application of MBTI to assist a community leadership program was really part of a larger strategy that: facilitated the networking of people in the community; helped participants work with large groups to accomplish major goals; assisted smaller teams in developing plans and executing projects; and improved the quality of life for everyone in the community.

The final illustration for the use of MBTI to improve organizational effectiveness is my work with a small company over the last 15 years. They are a privately owned company and have about 140 employees. I introduced MBTI to this organization in 2009 as a part of their annual strategic/operational planning process. The following is a description of ways they have utilized MBTI and some of the value they have gained. This is from the Assistant to the Owner/CEO:

"Our company began using Myers-Briggs as a tool more than ten years ago. It was initially used as a tool to help employees see themselves in relation to those with whom we were collaborating.

We had every employee take the Myers-Briggs Type Indicator and with their permission published the results for the purpose of improving business communications. We added the information to our list of employee email addresses and extension numbers, so it was readily accessible to anyone when they were contacting a colleague. We learned that being aware of the personality of the person with whom you were about to have a dialogue helped manage your expectations of the conversation.

During a department's weekly meeting, the supervisor's *Extraverted* personality gave the impression his position on issues was inflexible due the confidence with which he expressed ideas. He would often leave the meeting frustrated because no one else voiced an opinion about the topics covered. The MBTI training helped that supervisor realize his group was strongly *Introverted,* and they needed time to process the information. He began issuing an agenda for the meeting listing the topics for discussion and what kind of information he needed from them. This solved the problem. His staff came prepared to discuss the topics because he had given them time to process and gather information before the meeting.

It was evident that the owner who is a *"P"* surrounded himself with *"J"* type personalities to ensure his ideas were implemented. MBTI also made the executive team aware of the lack of diversity in areas, and they made a conscious decision to make hiring choices that would enhance the "personality pool." That was not a matter of hiring someone with a specific MBTI type but looking for people who had demonstrated the missing capability.

We sometimes hear conversations between employees reminding each other that the person they are about to approach is a certain type and therefore has a certain need. This has helped defuse frustrations based on someone's expectations of another person. They really do put into practice the concepts they learned.

Each year our annual retreats focused less time on MBTI, but there is always a basic review and reminder about how helpful it is to understand what to expect when communicating with co-workers with a different personality."

As you can see MBTI helped this organization in areas of communication, decision-making, leadership, and providing a framework for better understanding different perspectives. They also were able to recognize perspectives which might be missing and how to compensate for those gaps.

Hope these illustrations demonstrate the value of using MBTI from an organizational perspective to address a variety of issues impacting organizational performance. Here are suggestions about ways you can optimize the value of MBTI in your organization.

1. Identify internal or external resources with the capability of training employees and leaders in the proper use of MBTI concepts and consulting with leadership on application of MBTI in the following areas: communications, customer service, teamwork, decision-making, strategic planning, conflict resolution, change management, and other organizational applications.

2. Have employees take the MBTI and provide training on MBTI for all employees.

3. Conduct team workshops to improve teamwork and help teams understand the value of MBTI in improving relationships.

4. Utilize MBTI as an intervention tool as appropriate to address organizational issues like decision-making, conflict resolution, strategic planning, and resistance to change.

5. Assign responsibility to an organizational development person within the organization with MBTI capability to recognize potential applications of MBTI to organizational performance issues.

6. Provide all employees with a copy of this book. OK, that was self-serving. One colleague who reviewed *Power of Understanding* before I sent it to publishers told me the book really brought MBTI to life. He had read other excellent books on MBTI, but, for him, they did not illustrate the practical uses of MBTI with as many real life and relatable stories. Any material you provide employees on MBTI will be helpful. It is a worthwhile investment in their continual learning and will bear fruit in their personal and professional lives.

- **What:** The preferred behaviors of people in an organizational setting impact the culture and results of that organization.
- **So What:** By understanding preferred behavior through the MBTI lens, we can better understand potential root causes of personal and interpersonal issues which might be impacting organizational performance.
- **Now What:** Utilize MBTI to develop an organizational understanding of behavior within the organization and how it might be influencing culture and the results of the organization. Identify actions from that understanding to drive improvement in organizational culture and results.

CHAPTER 16

UNDERSTANDING
DIFFERENT TYPES

We have looked at how the individual preferences assist us in understanding why we and others respond in diverse ways to the following basic questions that determine a great deal about our behavior each day:

1. Do I go inside or outside myself for energy?
2. Do I perceive the world through my five senses or through hunches and possibilities?
3. Do I make decisions based on logic and reason or impact on people?
4. Do I organize and structure my life or observe and adapt to life?

By understanding my own response to these questions and the response of others, I can better accept and appreciate the responses of myself and others. Just knowing people's preferences is invaluable in enabling me to see an important perspective and avoid conflict because of very natural and understandable differences.

We have also considered how the interaction of preferences can help us understand different perspectives on key success factors in life, like decision-making, problem-solving, communications, and planning our lives. With this understanding, I can better leverage and play to my natural strengths while compensating for the things I do not do well. I can intentionally use certain processes or steps to ensure I do not overlook critical issues.

We have also examined the value of MBTI in certain critical areas like career decision-making, team-building, and personal/leadership development. Having spent over 30 years of my life doing work in these areas, it is hard for me to imagine how I would have been able to provide the type of assistance I sought to provide without MBTI as a tool.

In this chapter, we will explore the behaviors associated with the 16 Myers-Briggs types. These sixteen combinations of the four preferences create sixteen different personality types. The four-letter types describe what those combinations look like in terms of personal characteristics.

In my workshops, I focus on making sure participants understand the basics about how to use MBTI and what the preferences measure. We also look at the dynamics of MBTI and how the interaction of the letters will influence our preferred responses in situations. The workshops conclude with a review of the sixteen types and a discussion of the characteristics of the types. A lot of time is not devoted to a deep exploration of the sixteen types. In reviewing the types, I encourage participants to begin a journey of exploring their type as they gain a better understanding of MBTI concepts. Fortunately, there are a lot of resources which can help people learn more about MBTI.

To explore the sixteen types here, I would like to first provide a table that has a brief description of each type and the possible careers each type often pursues. This is to provide a quick overview of the types before we provide a more detailed example of each type.

16 MBTI Types and Brief Description

ISTJ	ISFJ	INFJ	INTJ
Very dependable & organized. Accounting, Administration	Very loyal, responsible, and reserved. Education, & Healthcare	Cares deeply and sees the world ideally. Religion & Counseling	Creative logical thinker & sees things differently. Technical.
ISTP	**ISFP**	**INFP**	**INTP**
Resourceful in realistically adapting. Military & skilled trades.	Observant & adaptive in a caring way. Healthcare & Law Enforce.	Empathetic and creative in caring deeply. Counseling & Writing	Independent in logical exploration. Research & Technical
ESTP	**ESFP**	**ENFP**	**ENTP**
Energetic and pragmatic responder. Business & Applied Tech.	Friendly and enthusiastic participant. Actor & Flight Attendant	Friendly with creative and active curiosity Journalism & Consulting	Creative, adaptive & analytical Entrepreneur & Marketing
ESTJ	**ESFJ**	**ENFJ**	**ENTJ**
Action bias using logic &, planning. Lawyer & Project Man.	Loyally cares for others in planned way. Healthcare & Education	Support others with energy and creativity. Public rel. & Trainer	Take charge & take logical, decisive action Management & Law

To provide a more detailed description of each type, I will describe a person for each type. Fourteen of these people are family members, friends, and work associates. I will not use a person's name unless the person is a family member. Each person has given me permission to use them in describing their type and have reviewed and approved what I have written. I will also use myself for my type.

The only person I will use that I do not know personally is Abraham Lincoln. I thought it would be interesting to use one famous person in helping us understand type. Obviously, it was impossible for President Lincoln to take the Myers-Briggs Type Indicator since the MBTI was developed after his tragic death. The four- letter type for President

Lincoln is what I have guessed his type to be based on his actions, his speeches, and other things we know about him from history. Once you develop a good understanding of the MBTI preferences you can become effective in determining other people's type.

I will start at the top left-hand side of the 16-type matrix and work to the right and down. We will begin our discussion of the sixteen types with *ISTJ*.

ISTJ
(Very dependable and organized)

ISTJs are the opposite of me (*ENFP*) on every preference and I have shared about how this has created challenges over the years because I have had several managers with this type. However, I have learned to value how they can enrich everything I do because they see things and do things which are a challenge for me to see or do.

As a result, I could have chosen a lot of different people for the *ISTJ* type, but I chose to look at a gentleman who has been the Chief Information Technology Officer for Company B. He has been in that role for over 20 years, and under his leadership, Company B has been a leader in their business sector, and they have won awards for their utilization of IT applications.

ISTJs often are in management roles. If you recall we discussed the "*TJ*" corners of the matrix, and how these corners are called the management domain. Research has shown that the percentage of *TJs* in management is typically twice the percentage of *TJs* in the general population.

This *ISTJ* leads an *INTJ* group, which is not unusual for an information technology group. His group is very innovative in providing IT solutions for the needs of Company B. Their leader does not allow the "let's keep it" mindset which often goes with *ISs* to limit doing things differently. His *IS* does place of importance on reliability which is critical in the day-to-day operations of Company B. There is a high expectation of taking care of every member they serve every time. This means making sure systems work in a way that enables the organization to achieve excellent member service is a top priority. This is a clear expectation of this *ISTJ*.

I observed his high expectation for precision in a humorous way one day. I was teaching a leadership course, and the room in which I was teaching had a new overhead projector installed in the ceiling along with other updated equipment. A member of the IT group had checked me out on the equipment, and I was ecstatic. The quality of slides, videos, and sound was dramatically better. As I was preparing for class the next morning, I noticed the *ISTJ* leader coming in the building along with one of the IT employees. They came into my classroom and the *ISTJ* leader asked me how the new equipment was working. I shared with him how happy I was with it. I had a slide up on a large screen in the front of the class and he looked at the slide, turned to the IT employee and said the image was slightly off in the lower right-hand corner. It was off about a quarter of an inch on screen that was about 8 ft. by 6 ft. I would have never noticed that small detail, but the *ISTJ* did. This high expectation for accuracy and precision is part of what makes him so effective in a role where accuracy and dependability are so important.

An important thing about this *ISTJ* is his ability to utilize his strengths in a way which contributes to his area of responsibility excelling at meeting the operational needs of Company B and the needs of its employees and members. He also recognizes what could limit his effectiveness. Since he is an *Introvert* and leads a group that are primarily *Introverts*, he is very deliberate about ensuring he and his group communicates with the rest of the organization. He has set up processes to ensure effective communications. In addition, he is open with the fact that communications might be something they will fail to do at times. He openly asks people to hold IT accountable for communicating adequately and provide them feedback if they do not.

His *SJ* could present a challenge in seeking out innovative ideas and being open to change. However, as I mentioned, his group has more people whose preference is *Intuition*. He has surrounded himself with strong people with different perspectives. He is also aware of the importance of being open to innovative ideas in a rapidly evolving field like IT.

Finally, his "*T*" does not prevent him from placing a great deal of importance on the impact of decisions and action upon people. This attention on the people impact comes from his maturity as a leader. Certainly, the corporate culture at Company B, which values positive treatment of people, reinforces use of an "*F*" perspective by everyone. Service to members and serving each other as employees is the most dominant value in Company B. Even if you have a preference for *Thinking*, you must learn to exercise your *Feeling* in Company B.

ISFJ
(Very loyal, responsible, and reserved)

The *ISFJ* I have chosen is a former work associate with Company A. We worked together in various capacities over my 28-year career with Company A, and he was my manager for three of my last four years with the company. He was a VP of Human Resources which was a predominantly *ISTJ* organization. He was an *F* in a *T* organization with a strong engineering influence and commitment to the importance of fairness, applying principles consistently, and complying with labor laws.

As an Industrial Engineer himself, over his 37 years with Company A he learned to navigate those *Thinking* dominant HR waters quite well. He served in a broad range of functions within HR and demonstrated capability in using his *IS* to maintain stability and effectiveness in managing those HR functions.

He used his *J* to execute plans in a manner which met or exceeded expectations, and he made decisions in a timely manner. Tasks were performed precisely, and you always knew what to expect from him.

The major difference I saw in this *ISFJ* leader and most leaders in HR was his willingness to do things uniquely in response to the individual need of employees. That was not the norm in HR. The assignment where I saw this demonstrated most was when he was responsible for international HR services. International HR involved unique situations constantly. We had employees from many different countries. We had U.S. based employees who relocated to other countries for temporary assignments. Labor laws in those countries were different. Salary structures in those countries were different. The need for consistency with our company's HR practices was critical as we sought to attract and retain people in these important international assignments. This *ISFJ* managed those challenges beautifully and became a valued contributor to the company in this role. He was able to satisfy HR management who placed a high value on company-wide equity and at the same time satisfy a very culturally diverse group of manufacturing, sales, and supply chain managers.

Company A was expanding internationally in a significant way during this time. I believe this manager's strength of considering the impact of actions on individuals and finding ways to meet unique needs contributed to the success of those international growth efforts.

As my manager we were different on three of the four letters and shared only the "*F*" in common. I loved working for him because he respected the unique abilities associated with my type, and I respected and valued his abilities based on his type. He reined me in at times by raising practical realities which the *IS* sees clearly. The important thing was the reining in did not come in the form of "no we can't do this." Instead, it was "Rick, here are potential obstacles I see. How can we deal with that?" It seemed like the synergy in our types enabled us to overcome most of those obstacles.

Our shared "*F*" enabled us to focus energy on engaging employees. We were able to work with his team to do different things in support of management's effort to enable employees to feel like valued partners in our businesses and not just employees. I was also able to work as an OD facilitator with a senior leadership team on which he participated, and it was truly one of the most rewarding experiences in my work career. It was special because of the relationships, and he was a major contributor to that.

INFJ
(Cares deeply and sees the world ideally)

For the *INFJ*, I have chosen my daughter, Kelly. You might want to read each of this with a hint of skepticism because I believe my daughter is wonderful. However, all the people I have chosen except one are people I know well and admire. I believe MBTI has helped me see them accurately and realistically.

With my daughter, her MBTI preferences were apparent early. I have already discussed as a part of reviewing the *E/I* preference how you could see her clear preference for *I* as a small child. This preference has remained clear throughout her life. She has maintained a small network of close friends. She still loves reading. As a college professor, which is a good fit for an *INFJ*, she loves going deep into her areas of expertise.

You could also see her *F* early in life. She was a caretaker with her little brother and was fearless in standing up for others. I remember her confronting a group of guys who were picking on her younger brother when he started high school. She let them know they better stop, or they would have to deal with her. She did not tolerate mistreatment of the "little guy" or anyone for that matter.

Kelly paved her own way. Whether it was being in a movie with Sissy Spacek and Mel Gibson, doing community theatre, or playing volleyball in college, she loved trying new things. She never sweated the details. She was all about trying new things and she was open to taking big leaps and did not use a step-by-step approach to life. I remember one summer when she was eight years-old we were at the University of Tennessee outdoor pool. Kelly had been jumping off the high diving board which was Olympic height. It was a Saturday, and I told her if she would jump off the platform dive, which was thirty-three feet high, we would eat at her favorite restaurant after church the next day. Without hesitation, she started walking toward the platform. I thought "oh my goodness she's going to do it." I jumped up and followed her, because I feared she would climb the ladder to the top of the platform and get scared. Well, she climbed the ladder with me behind her and walked straight to the edge and jumped off. In amazement, I thought to myself: "Well, you have to jump off now." Kelly was always ready for new things.

Her *J* has been much more evident in her adult life, and I see it in spades in her roles as a mother and coach. In addition to teaching at a university, she coached volleyball at her university for two years and at a high school for six years. With her children, she is the planner/coordinator in making sure all the things are scheduled and completed. She also brought that same structure and discipline to her coaching. Her *F* is the most dominant thing you see in her as a mother and coach. She cares deeply for those under her guidance and care. But she also focused on the things they needed to do to reach the goals they were working toward.

There are two areas I have seen my daughter struggle with at times, and they are both easy to understand in terms of her type. The first is an issue associated with the combination of the *N* and *J*. Kelly has achieved a great deal in her life. Graduating with high honors, getting two graduate degrees, being named state coach of the year in her division, and being a cancer survivor. I am not sure she experiences the full joy of that because *N*s produce so many things they want to accomplish and feel frustrated as *J*s when they do not achieve them all. I think at times she is too hard on herself.

Secondly, at times those incredible ideas she generates with the *IN* creativity do not get out into the external world because, for her, the energy is satisfied inside. Since she is an *I*, getting the idea out into the external world needs to be intentional, because it is not natural.

Her compassionate and idealistic drive is consistent with her *INFJ* type. These traits are perfect for the roles she has played as a minister's wife, college professor at a wonderful Christian university, a mentor to young women in Sunday School and sports, and as a mother to two wonderful young adults. She is an incredible daughter too who helps to keep her dad out of trouble.

INTJ
(Creative, logical and sees things differently)

For *INTJ*, I will use my last manager at Company A. He became my manager a year before I retired from Company A. During my first three years at Company A, I worked in the compensation area with many of the people with who I would continue to work when I returned ten years later. This manager came to work while I was away from Company A. We got to know each other when I returned, but our careers in Human Resources were never in the same area. I always heard good things about him and grew to respect him based on the interactions we had on rare occasions.

In my new role, I gradually realized how fortunate I was to be facing the uncertainty of this change with this *INTJ* leader. My work from the time I returned to Company A had been in areas which were not the core of Human Resources. I had no desire for an assignment in those areas. This *INTJ* manager, whose strengths were strategic planning, seeing the big picture, and being highly analytical, was able to carve out a unique role which was needed at that time. That role utilized my strengths very well.

The Human Resources leadership team was going through significant changes and so I became a facilitator for that team while working with the Sr. VP for Human Resources, Communications, and Public Affairs. In addition, there was a need to do a better job of communicating to employees the value proposition which Company A was offering to employees. I was given the responsibility of leading a team in developing a clear definition of that value proposition and communicating it to managers in a way they could communicate to employees.

In performing those two roles, this *INTJ* used his strengths in a significant way to guide the work I was doing. The changes that the company and HR were going through were driven by significant changes in the management team, challenging business conditions, technology, and a tough economy. Maintaining the status quo was not an option. This manager's *IN* enabled him to explore new directions while being open to new ways of doing things which were not necessarily the norm for HR.

In addition, his tough *TJ* management perspective was critical in exploring options which made business sense. Anything else would not have been acceptable for the business environment in which we found ourselves.

It is also interesting that the traditional background of leaders in HR at Company A was industrial engineering. This HR VP had a B.S. in chemistry, and an MBA. This analytical and more visionary educational background was very normal for his type and excellent preparation for the role he ended up playing in Company A.

ISTP
(Resourceful in realistically adapting)

The person I will use to describe the *ISTP* type is the Director of Facilities for Company B, and if you consider the adjectives that are often used to describe an *ISTP*, it is very apparent her type is perfect for the role she plays.

The word spontaneous is another characteristic of an *ISTP* and if you are managing almost thirty facilities housing about nine hundred employees in three states which serve 240,000 members. There are many situations which arise each day requiring spontaneous action needed to keep operations going. It could be electricity, phone lines, plumbing, and any problem associated with inhabiting a building. You cannot put those repairs on a list and get to them next week. Those repairs need to be completed quickly, and this person leads a team that ensures those buildings are functional, attractive, and a safe place for people to conduct business each day.

The word resourceful describes an *ISTP*, and it is important for a director of facilities to be good at finding the labor, materials, and funds needed to respond to any issue that arises. There are competing demands that arise unexpectedly. Having the flexibility to respond to those demands in the heat of the moment is a valuable talent in this role. A major example of the importance of being resourceful was during Covid. To do business safely, many changes in facilities like transparent plastic screens for tellers and others dealing directly with members had to be installed quickly.

Realistic is also a major characteristic of *ISTPs*. This along with being very data driven and logical makes it easy for this person to remain calm when everyone around her thinks the sky is falling. She remains calm and communicates the realities of the situation in a very factual manner. Emotions will not take over, because she will let you know the realities of the situation and the plan for dealing with the situation.

This organization has grown rapidly over the last 20 years. The adventuresome spirit of an *ISTP* has served this person well in being quite willing to tackle the facilities challenges associated with that growth.

It is also quite appropriate that *ISTPs* often choose skilled trades for a career. As a director of facilities, this person negotiates and manages contracts with companies whose employees are primarily people from the skilled trades. She is comfortable working with people from this field because their personalities are similar.

As I have observed this person function over the years, she has always seemed unflappable. I believe a lot of that is because there is such a strong match of her personality with the demands of her job.

ISFP
(Observant and adaptive in caring way)

At times in MBTI workshops, I am asked, "what personality type is the most likely to be a good listener?" I respond with *ISFP*. *Introverts* are usually better listeners than *Extraverts* because the *E* wants to tell you the thought they are having, while the *Introvert* focuses their attention on what you are saying. The *Sensing* person lives in the moment and so they are present with you and gathering the details of what you are sharing. The person whose preference is *Intuition* listens to your first thought and jumps to the possibilities associated with what you are saying. The *Feeling* person is concerned about how what you are saying will the impact your life, while the *Thinking* person is looking at the logic of what you are saying. And finally, the *Perceiving* person is curious and likes to understand what you are saying, while the *Judging* person often jumps to a conclusion before they hear you out.

The person I will use to help us understand the *ISFP* type is my wife, Marcie, and she is an excellent listener. She is so good at listening to understand people in a deeper way. She has a wonderful ability to understand beyond the content of the words. She has this ability because she uses each of her preferences as described in the previous paragraph.

As described in the chapter on Career Decision-Making, Marcie's top career match was a nun in the Catholic order. I believe the *ISFP* quality of caring is why this was her top career match. I know I may be biased, but I tell people my wife is one of the kindest people I have ever known, and I have been fortunate to know many truly kind people. Marcie cares deeply about others whether she knows them or not. Tears are not unusual when we watch a tragic situation described on the news. When someone we know is in need, Marcie always wants to discuss what we can do to help. Her *Feeling* is her dominant preference, and you can see this in the depth of her caring for family, friends, and people in general.

That sensitivity to the need of others is so characteristic of *ISFPs*. People who go into healthcare are often this type and Marcie managed a medical practice for 20 years. Her major contribution was ensuring a focus on taking care of the total person. Anytime a patient was unhappy with their care, a bill, or anything, the staff brought the situation to Marcie, and she would talk with the patient. The patients would go away satisfied. The staff jokingly called her the "schmoozer" because Marcie would make everyone happy regardless of how upset they were initially. Two definitions of schmoozer are: 1) to converse in-order-to gain an advantage; 2) to make a social connection. Marcie's "schmoozing" was not about gaining an advantage. It was about making a social connection. She has that wonderful ability to let someone know she hears their concern, is taking it seriously, and will do everything she can to address the concern.

Modesty is a characteristic of this type, and she goes about life with such humility. She is never threatening to anyone. She instills trust with people she has just met, and I am constantly amazed at how people she has never known before share things with her they have not shared with anyone.

The final characteristic of the *ISFP* which is so evident with Marcie is how observant she is. I saw this in a dramatic way as we cared for my mother. Mom lived with us for the last five years of her life and was active until her last few months. I knew my mother well, and I am good at recognizing people's needs. However, Marcie would see things I would miss. It could be a body movement or tone of Mom's voice or a change in Mom's routine. Marcie recognized the little signals that something was wrong. She was truly the ultimate caregiver.

I do think my wife is close to a saint, but I know she is not perfect. The thing we struggle with most now is our similarity on the *J/P* preference. Since we are both *Perceiving*, we at times neglect the work-related activities at home. In teaching the *J/P* preferences, I use an exercise where I put a sign saying, "Work Before Play" on one wall, and on the opposite wall I put a sign saying, "Play Before Work." I then place myself in the middle and ask class participants to stand in the position that best describes their view in relation to work and play. It is amazing how those who are *Judging* always stand closer to the "Work Before Play" and those who are *Perceiving* always stand closer to the "Play Before Work." My wife and I both prefer to play, and we really enjoy it. We both must exert effort to get those day-to-day chores in life done.

INFP
(Empathetic and creative in caring deeply)

The person I am choosing as an example of the *INFP* type was initially a work associate at Company A and then became a dear friend. One of my first experiences with him was doing a MBTI workshop with his group when he was Director of Corporate Strategy for the company.

His role was a great fit for this *INFP*. People with the preferences of *INP* are great researchers and think about things very differently, so it is natural for them to focus on the future and think strategically. They are very imaginative and good at considering new paths for accomplishing desired results.

Someone involved in business research and strategic planning will normally have a preference for *Thinking* instead of *Feeling*, especially if that strategic planning role is for a large chemical company. Instead, this person's decision-making preference is *F*, and we will look at how that played out in his career in a moment. This person was obviously quite effective in using his lesser preferred *T* because he had a bachelors and masters-of-science degrees in chemical engineering. In addition, he had an MBA, so he was quite capable in the areas of analysis and reasoning.

However, it was the use of his *Feeling* that stood out to me as I got to know him. As we worked together in the area of leadership development, I began to realize he saw himself as more of a mentor than a director of corporate strategy. His group became a feeder for business leaders within the company. More people advanced to director or officer level positions after working in his group than any other group within the company.

This development of people became a passion for him. He took the company's employee development system and put it on steroids. Many managers complained about the employee development system and how it did not work. Most employees did not like it. He used the same system, executed it flawlessly, and his employees loved it. The problem was not with the system or process. The problem was the lack of commitment to developing people on the part of many managers. This *INFP* had a commitment to help others grow which is a characteristic of this type.

He came to me once and wanted to add a 360-degree feedback process to the development system for his employees. A 360-degree feedback process involves getting feedback from four different perspectives, thus the concept of 360 degrees. The four sources were most typically: yourself, your manager, your colleagues, and either the people you lead or your customers. This feedback usually is a rating on certain work behaviors/skills and comments. This *INFP* manager felt the feedback would be useful in helping his employees see their strengths and areas for development. He would then collaborate with them in finding ways to better utilize their strengths and improve where needed.

The primary reason this process worked was his role modeling how to use the feedback to improve. He did a 360 himself and then reviewed the results with his group. He shared the good, the bad, and the ugly. He acknowledged areas in which he needed improvement and even sought their input for specific ways he could do better. It blew his employees away that he was willing to share his needs for improvement. His behavior was an example which motivated the team to be the best they could be. This process worked because his employees would move into jobs which involved promotions because this *INFP* made sure they had opportunities to show their capabilities.

As a result, he had high turnover because people were quickly selected for better opportunities. However, good people were standing in line to get into his group because he had a reputation as a developer of leaders. On his LinkedIn page today, he identifies him as "Retired Mentor." This is not a surprise for an *INFP*. However, a mentor is never quite retired. He continues to mentor younger people with whom he interacts.

INTP
(Independent in logical exploration)

For the *INTP*, I want to use a famous person instead of someone I have known personally. To explore the *INTP* type, we will look at the life of Abraham Lincoln, who many believe to be an *INTP*.

Two words often associated with *INTPs* are autonomous and original. Both characteristics certainly apply to Lincoln, and he was most definitely original. Considered by many to be our country's greatest president, he was a unique person. His physical image, dress and persona make him easily distinguishable when compared to others. What he accomplished from very humble beginnings is quite incredible.

Autonomous is another word to describe Lincoln and he was certainly that. In his early years as an adult, he was a shopkeeper, postmaster, and eventually general store owner. He demonstrated his leadership ability by being elected captain by volunteers at the age of twenty-three when the Black Hawk War broke out. Shortly after that he started in politics. He was elected to the Illinois House of Representatives at the age of twenty-five. During this period, he began to pursue becoming a lawyer. He taught himself by reading law books and became a lawyer in 1837. Now that is autonomy.

As our President, he confronted two of the greatest challenges our country has ever faced. One was the issue of the union or our form of governance, and the other was whether slavery would continue, which

Lincoln saw as a moral issue. *INs* think deeply and differently about things and Lincoln's ideas related to these two issues set our country on a path which has shaped who we are as a country as much as anyone including the founding fathers. Even as he ran for Senate before becoming President he said, "A house divided cannot stand." His position was the Union must survive. Later at Gettysburg, President Lincoln drew from the Declaration of Independence in declaring: "Government of the people, by the people, for the people, shall not perish from the earth." He continued by stating this Union was "dedicated to the proposition that all men are created equal." Lincoln's vision was for this more perfect union where one person did not own another. He was a true visionary in seeing the possibility in those inspiring words and being relentless in pursuing them.

The *Thinking* preference served him well. For *Ts*, justice is an important guiding principle in making decisions. *Ts* weigh the evidence like the pros and cons of any issue. Lady Justice is a common symbol of justice in U.S. courthouses. Lady Justice is blindfolded to convey impartiality. She carries a sword to demonstrate there is punishment when found guilty. She holds scales to represent the weight of evidence in determining justice. All the evidence is weighed, and the result determines guilt or innocence. I believe Lincoln studied, reflected deeply, and weighed all the evidence in making the moral determination that slavery must be abolished.

Once he came to that conclusion and set upon a course of keeping the Union together and abolishing slavery, the opposition and challenges were incredible. But the issue was settled and clear in his mind. *Ts* find that type of clarity in justice. He was tough minded and never wavered. He recognized the challenges he faced and surrounded himself with a cabinet made up of former political rivals. He was not afraid to be challenged and believed diversity of thought was a major asset of his first term in office.

As a person with the preference of *Perceiving*, he had an incredible ability to adapt. No President faced a more immediate threat to the survival of our country. But despite serving only a month over four years, his response to that crisis is primarily responsible for maintaining the unity of our country and freeing a group of people from the travesty of slavery. He was a true visionary.

ESTP
(Energetic and pragmatic responder)

To illustrate the *ESTP* type, I am choosing someone I worked with briefly over a period of three years. She was an event planner, and my friend, Zellie, and I collaborated with her on a few big corporate training events. We had two major officers' retreats at Company A over a two-year period, and we did some teambuilding events overseas. This lady worked with us to plan all the logistics for those meetings. About seventy people would attend the officers' retreats, and the activities included complex games and business simulations. We would collaborate with external consultants and others to plan activities designed to reach the learning objectives of the CEO.

The common type for event planners is *ESFJ*, because the event planner is focused on making people happy while insuring all the arrangements are scheduled and completed as planned. This is what *ESFJs* do. But this *ESFP* was incredible for us to work with because so much of the success of these retreats depended on how the simulations and activities evolved as we went through the retreat. Her adaptability was where this event planner excelled.

Her *E* ensured everyone was aware of the critical logistical information. Her *S* ensured the vital details were attended to as we planned and executed the retreats. Her *T* enabled her to be unflappable because she was very pragmatic in responding to problems and was quick to find solutions. Her combination of *E* and *S* brought a positive "let's do it" energy to everything we threw her way.

The type of training events we were conducting utilized "experiential learning," which means you design simulated experiences for people to carry out with a learning objective in mind. You cannot predict exactly what will happen with these exercises. The incredible thing about experiential learning is it leads to an outcome which achieves the learning objective despite this uncertainty. However, these exercises are not for the faint at heart because they seldom go exactly as planned. Experiential learning activities can drive people crazy. However, this type of learning can bring about an awareness of how we behave and what the outcome of that behavior is.

This type of learning is difficult to achieve in a classroom setting. Zellie and I had considerable experience with these learning activities and loved the way they could go in many directions. Since this event planner was a *P*, she got it and was comfortable making the plans needed, while also maintaining the willingness to adapt on the run when something changed.

For me, this was a great lesson about the importance of finding the best match of type for a given situation.

ESFP
(Friendly and enthusiastic participant)

To describe the *ESFP*, I will use my son, Chris. An *ESFP* is the ultimate people person. *Extraverts* are energized by interactions with people and being involved in activities. As a *Sensing* person, they live in the moment and are truly present with you. The *Feeling* preference results in them always considering how things impact the people around them. And finally, their *Perceiving* enables them to go with the flow and adapt easily to people and situations. They do not get locked into an agenda.

With my son, these characteristics are certainly very evident in his life. He loves doing things with others. As a teacher, coach, minister, and friend, his focus on active involvement with others is the defining characteristic in his life. He is always doing something with someone.

He builds relationships easily and they endure. It is not part of a plan, but it happens in a wonderful spontaneous manner.

His career choices match very well with his type and even his love of acting and sports early in his life fit his type well. He played the lead in a community theatre musical and performed in other plays and one movie as an extra. He won several speech contests as a child and is comfortable "performing" in front of people.

He was always very tolerant and accepting of others. I can recall in middle school how a young lady, who was a good friend, had done something which some of the other youth judged to be wrong. While others rejected her, Chris was very intentional about continuing to be her friend. He did not agree with what she had done, but strictly following the rules was something he believed none of us did perfectly. It was very natural for him to be accepting of her in-spite of her behavior. That quality has enabled him to maintain very long-term friendships because perfection is not required in those relationships.

His active involvement with others is observable in very practical ways. It could be about helping a hitter in volleyball contact the ball at the exact best point. It might be about helping a tennis player follow through correctly on their forehand. It could potentially be about helping a young person in a youth group know what they can do to help repair a broken friendship. His focus is on the practical things he can do to help someone.

Another way I see this practical approach to life and relationships is his gift giving. He is a great gift giver. His gifts are always based on things he has observed which provide a clear indication of the gift you will love. The gift idea flows from an impression about something Chris knows you love because he has seen or heard you express a passion that points to the gift.

I often run into someone who has met Chris through one of his activities. It could be school, work, sports, church, or just a network of friends. Without exception, when they discover I am Chris' dad, their response is "I love Chris Toomey," and you can tell the response is genuine because that person will go on and talk about how they know Chris. Many things explain that response to Chris, but I believe his *ESFP* type plays a role. *ESFPs* are some of the most fun-loving people you will ever meet. I loved taking him and friends to do things when he was growing up and seeing the sheer joy of their friendship. I have been fortunate as an adult to be involved in activities with Chris and his friends and see the depth of those friendships.

Fs can be driven by the need to please people and find themselves lost in their desire to please others. I have observed Chris grow in this area over the years. I know he has a desire to please people and make them happy and he does that very well. Jung defines maturity as learning to use the non-preferred preference and I have observed Chris channel his *F* very effectively without letting it drive every decision. At times, I have seen him use tough love as a coach, teacher, minister, and leader. It is not always easy for him, but he knows it is important to do in certain situations.

Chris and I were driving in Louisville, KY one day, while visiting my sister. I had lived in Louisville for about a year and was familiar with the area and Chris had been there before. We were driving along a busy four-lane road and were approaching a freeway that we needed to get on going north. I asked Chris if he remembered whether we needed to be in the left or right lane to get on the ramp. Chris' response was "I don't recall Dad, but we can always turn around and come back." For two people with a preference for *Perceiving*, this is not a problem at all because for them life is about adapting and not having to get everything right the first time every time.

Chris is a great adapter, but I have seen him, over the years, gain the ability to develop and execute a plan very well. His work at times demands it and his personal life, at times, benefits from it. He has played to the strengths of his *P* very well while learning to use his *J* as needed.

ENFP

(Friendly with creative and active curiosity)

I have used family, friends, work associates, and one famous person so far to explore what the four- letter types look like. For this one, I will try to describe the *ENFP* by looking at myself. I have certainly lived about fifty of my 75 years knowing my type and trying to use that understanding to help me be more effective as a person. It has certainly been helpful in explaining why I fail and mess up at times. It has also helped me understand why some things work really work for me.

As I mentioned in the chapter on career decision-making, the careers I have been blessed to work in for fifty of my fifty-three adult years are good matches for my MBTI type. That helps to explain why I love my work. Work has enabled me to channel my creativity, expressiveness, and curiosity in efforts to develop people in innovative and interactive ways.

The restlessness that is often a characteristic of my type has led me to take on many distinct roles and work assignments over the years. I have been in fourteen different work-related roles over those 50 years. Once I master something at a certain level, I tend to want to move on to another challenge. That has worked well for me, but that restlessness can create problems for those around me at times.

Another major characteristic of *ENFPs* is idealism. We can set standards that are at times impossible to meet. As *Ps*, we are accustomed to not completing everything we start and things not always going as planned. But at times, I have been guilty of setting what might be unreasonable expectations for others. Making sure others understand the goal set is an aspiration and not an expectation is something I must keep in mind. I set goals for myself and often achieve those and frequently in a circuitous and creative manner as opposed to a defined plan. I do not achieve all those goals and for me that is OK because *Ps* are accustomed to that. It is important for me to be clear with the people in my life that it is OK with me if they do not achieve the goals also.

My idealism combined with the passion I have for something and my desire to influence others to have the same enthusiasm can be unfair to others. Unless I am willing to be realistic and execute my part of the plan to get there, I am creating energy for something which may be unrealistic. This can set others up for disappointment. For this reason I have grown to value people who are different from me because they help me ensure I utilize my strengths in a positive way and not in a way which creates problems for others. One valued work associate who happened to be an ESTJ jokingly shared this about me at a retreat for the elders of our church: "Rick Toomey can think of more things for other people to do than anyone I've ever known." He was right. My strength is generating ideas and possibilities and being a catalyst for getting others involved in accomplishing something. It is important for me to make sure others have the same enthusiasm for the path forward. I need to ensure they know the agreed path is in their best interest, and they agree it is possible and something they want to sign up for.

My *Intuition* and *Feeling* have enabled me to empathize with people and connect events in their lives to feelings they are experiencing. This has been invaluable in my roles as a minister, counselor, and teacher. Helping people see patterns in their lives and use that understanding to break away from behaviors that are counterproductive and develop constructive responses in situations has been a major focus in my life. That has been immensely rewarding. The tough thing has been to see those patterns and not being able to help people recognize them and then having to observe the negative outcomes. This anticipation of what is going to happen is not perfect. I am occasionally wrong and when a bad outcome does not occur, I am relieved. However, it does happen enough that it brings frequent disappointment. A plus side of this natural strength is I can anticipate good things happening for people, when at times they do not believe it. Being able to then celebrate with them is wonderful. Our strengths have an upside and a downside. McKenzie Management talks about a "strength overused can become a weakness." This is so true with our MBTI preferences and type.

ENTP

(Creative, adaptive, and analytical)

To describe the *ENTP*, I will use a gentleman who became an Executive Vice-President at Company A. He retired from a role which involved managing about half of the company's business and all the functions involved with those businesses. I knew him for about 25 years of his employment with Company A and had the opportunity to work with him very closely during the last four years of his employment. My role was the Organizational Development Manager for that part of the organization, and I also served as a facilitator for his team.

A part of my role was to provide he and his team with feedback on the way their decisions and plans would impact people. Since he had a clear preference for *Thinking* and his team was very dominant in *T*, he was aware his team might neglect to consider the impact of decisions and actions upon people. Despite leading with an analytical and bottom-line approach in decision-making, he understood the importance of having strong employee buy-in and support for decisions. He knew decisions had to be in their best interest. He was intent on making sure his team's decisions were in the best interest of employees and those decisions were effectively communicated to employees.

He was a brilliant person in business and had served the company as CFO, leader of several businesses, sales management, marketing, and strategic planning. His *Thinking* served him well in all those roles. However, it was his awareness of the importance of involving people and genuinely valuing people that led him to become very adept at using *Feeling*. He sponsored programs like a business educational and alignment effort which involved senior leaders meeting with all employees in groups of about twenty to help them understand the financials of our businesses and what was important to the success of those businesses. He initiated the gift of a dinner for an employee and their family for special day-to-day contributions they made. Every manager had a budget for distributing these gifts any time they saw an employee making a significant contribution.

This *ENTP* leader once gave a dinner gift to two employees he saw at the airport coming back from a trip to one of our plants. They had gone there because of an unplanned shutdown of the plant. They had helped get the plant up and running in a way that minimized costs to the company. This leader saw them, discussed what they had done, and gave them a card to take their families out for a meal of their choice. This was a unique way to say thanks for the work they had done. Those employees told me about this chance meeting, and they were so appreciative of this simple recognition they received.

This leader's *Extroversion* was effective in engaging people and keeping them informed, which he believed was critical. He was great at building business relationships which served our company's interests well. He was also aware of how his *E* could dominate a discussion and that along with his high business acumen could be intimidating for people in expressing their views. One of his practices that minimized the chance that his *E* would prevent others from expressing their views was the way he presented his ideas in meetings. When a topic came up in a meeting, he would never express his opinion until everyone had expressed their viewpoint. If someone had not spoken, he would say, "John, I would really like to know how you see this." Once everyone had talked, if there seemed to be strong agreement about a course of action and it was close to his viewpoint, he would say something like, "I think that sounds great and I agree that is the course we need to pursue." If he did not agree, he might say something like, "I see the value in the direction you all are leaning toward but based on this factor, I want us to go in a different direction." He only did this when he was accountable for the decision, and he strongly believed his direction was the way we needed to go. His team accepted and supported those decisions, because they knew he always considered their viewpoint and, in most cases, accepted it as the direction chosen. In ways, this process was an exercise in exchanging ideas which is very energizing for an *ENTP*.

His *Intuition* was valuable in looking to the future. He was a strategic-thinker and was quite willing to challenge the status quo whether it was a long-held assumption about a business or HR practices. The *N* combined with his *Perception* could have created frustrations for people, especially those he managed. He could overwhelm others with a flurry of ideas and things to do. Fortunately, he understood this and really valued the *SJs* around him. They were the ones with whom he developed strong trusting relationships, because they were the ones he knew would "rein him in." They helped him understand the importance of the realities of a given situation and having a plan to address those realities.

This leader and *ENTPs* in general are known to stretch themselves, friends, work associates, and family. They see life situations as an opportunity to challenge yourself and grow. I observed this with this leader when the CEO of Company A retired. It was obvious to most people that the successor would either be him or one other gentleman in the company. When the *ENTP* leader was told he would not be the CEO and it would be announced the next day at 8 AM, he scheduled a meeting with his leadership team for 7 AM. As a member of the team, I recall we were disappointed, but he very quickly made us aware he fully accepted the decision and was confident the new CEO would do an excellent job. He expressed his full support for the decision. He shared with us what his role would be and that our team would continue to function in a way we were currently functioning. He also requested that we all fully support the new CEO and let everyone know he was happy with his role and looked forward to helping the company continue its success. He emphasized strongly that he did not want this to become a divisive decision. He proceeded to go out and be very visible with employees while demonstrating support for the new CEO. When people would say things like, "I think you should have been the CEO," he expressed his confidence and support of the new CEO. What incredible leadership!

Rather than allowing ego to take over, he saw this new challenge as a growth opportunity. This is a splendid example of being truly adaptive and learning through tough times and that is what *ENTPs* do.

ESTJ
(Action bias using logic and planning)

For the *ESTJ*, I am going to discuss the new CEO of Company B. She has been in that role for only five months as I write, but for her it has seemed much longer. It is May of 2020, and we are in the middle of the first pandemic since 1918.

This *ESTJ* is well suited for this challenge, both in terms of her professional preparation and her type. *ESTJs* are tough-minded and task driven. When faced with stay-at-home guidance and social distancing, she has led the organization in developing a decisive and well thought out plan. The plan will take care of member's needs, which is a major focus for this financial organization, while also keeping employees safe and financially secure.

It has been a tremendous challenge for companies to develop plans for dealing with a partial shut-down of the economy. Financial institutions were essential but had to observe certain guidelines. In response to those circumstances, these are some of the actions Company B took under the leadership of this *ESTJ*:

- They closed access to the branches except for scheduled walk-in business that could not be conducted by drive-through.
- Encouraged continued personal service via drive-through.

- Avoided temporary employee lay-offs by going to two six-hour shifts which also resulted in half of the staff being in a branch at a time. This facilitated social distancing.
- Enabled non-member contact employees to work from home as much as possible to enable them to be safer at home.

These changes enabled Company B to do the following: continue serving their members safely; provide continued employment and no loss of income for their employees; maintain operations in a financially viable manner; and protect the health of their employees and members. At this time, none of their employees have contracted the Coronavirus.

This is what *ESTJs* do. They tackle problems with a "let's do it" mindset. This *ESTJ* has done this her entire career. She has worked in most areas of Company B and has placed her thumbprint upon those areas. Over 15 years ago she led a team which developed a set of Service Excellence Expectations that continue to guide employees today. Those principles have practical and specific expectations about how employees interact with members and each other. I collaborated with the team in deploying those principles. They were committed to ensuring the principles did not become a document hanging on a wall but a set of real observable behaviors. During implementation of the expectations, they had an "expectation of the day," and this kept it constantly in front of employees. They encouraged people to check with employees to be sure they knew the expectation of the day. When I would go through a drive through station, I would ask the employee serving me what the expectation of the day was, and they could always tell me.

This *ESTJ* also led the Operations Team for many years, which involved managing over twenty branches and almost half of the employees. During that time, she coined a phrase to guide operations. The phrase was "every member, every time." It provided a simple reminder to our employees how critical it was to stay in the moment and focus on the member with whom you were interacting. *SJs* are all about paying attention to the details of the moment and completing each transaction as needed.

I have no doubt this *ESTJ* will provide the leadership needed to ensure the continued success of this financial institution which is among the top in its business sector. She has numerous natural strengths from which she can draw. Part of my confidence in her is based on observing how she compensates for areas which could be a problem for her. For example, she does not allow her *S* to limit her focus to the past and present. She has demonstrated her ability to lead rapid growth in the number of branches and to develop an aggressive growth plan in a new area. She also led three major areas of the organization as an Executive Vice-President in a very coordinated way for a year prior to becoming CEO.

Her *T* has never caused her to be only focused on logic and reason in making decisions. She has demonstrated that a *T* with an accounting background can embrace a culture with a strong focus on people and become effective at building and demonstrating a deep appreciation for how people are affected. The previous CEO told her when she assumed responsibility for operations it was all about the people. She talks frequently about how that simple advice helped her to realize in the end it was really all about the people.

This *ESTJ* has a good grasp of playing to her strengths and developing in areas which might not be as natural for her.

ESFJ
(Loyally cares for others in a planned way)

ESFJs are effective and gracious in dealing with others. When I reflect on this type, I think of nurses and elementary school teachers. For the *ESFJ*, we will consider a person who leads a training and development group at Company B.

To describe this *ESFJ*, I decided to do it through the eyes of the people she leads. I asked them the single question, "what is like to work for this person." Their responses do an incredible job of describing what *ESFJs* are like.

What is it like to work for this ESFJ?

Employee 1 (ISTJ):

It is a breath of fresh air. You know where you stand with her. She is fair to everyone. She is outgoing, which makes for enjoyable conversation, even to an *Introvert* like me. She is easy to talk to. She is supportive of any endeavors that I have, even the slightest of ideas. She is warm and genuinely cares about you as a person, not just as a co-worker. She cares about your immediate family too. She is always so helpful. Anytime I have ever needed assistance, she has been right there for me. She is not afraid to get in there and do the work too. That says so much about her as a manager.

I hope to be able to call her my manager for years to come.

Employee 2 (ESFJ):

If you know her, you automatically love her. Her kind and caring spirit is infectious. I have worked beside her as a co-worker and work with her today as my manager, and she still amazes me.

Here are the things that stand out to me about her.

- She is a firm believer in talking out any misunderstandings as quickly as possible to keep everyone on good terms with each other. This prevents allowing any negative feelings to grow or hinder relationships between coworkers of any kind, and results in a more harmonious work environment.
- She is a hugger—so be prepared if she has not seen you in a while—you will get a hug (if she knows you). This leaves every-

one she encounters feeling cared for (and she truly does care for everyone she knows). And if you are hurting, she is always there to offer a loving hug to let you know she is there to support you in any way she can, and she means that with all her heart.

- Since she used to be a trainer, she knows almost everyone. If she sees you in the hall, she will always ask how you are doing—not just to be courtesy, but because she genuinely cares how you are doing (and yes, you will likely get a hug too).
- She tackles a multitude of tasks daily but is willing to stop at any given moment if you need to ask her a question—no matter if it is fifty times in a day.
- She supports you at every turn, but if you are on the wrong track, she will quickly steer you back on course to ensure you present your best.
- When preparing to launch a new training program, she looks at how the sessions we offer will affect the branches, such as:
  - Are we offering enough sessions to keep the branches staffed?
  - Are the times we have chosen going to allow staff to get to the training facility in time, in relation to branch staffing (considering vacations and lunches)?
  - Does the training overlap any other items that require staff's time and attention?
- She always has other people's best interest at heart.
- She can respectfully disagree with someone if they have completely different views. Most of the time, she can find common ground to eliminate a full-on disagreement.
- She looks for the good in all people.
- She is always smiling and always positive.

She is truly one of those people who makes the world a better place just by being in it, and I consider myself blessed to know her. She is one of my all-time favorite people on the planet, and I love her dearly.

Employee 3 (ENFJ):

She becomes very invested in her co-workers and direct reports. I would say in my observations, it is this characteristic that has allowed her to build a high performing team. In my experience, she has taken the time to understand my personality, aspirations, and communication style. In short, she has taken the time to get to know me. This type of personal leadership allows for open communication and a desire, in turn, to help her succeed. The relationships she cultivates are mutually driven.

She was a catalyst, spurring my decision to go back to college as a non-traditional working adult. Throughout the entire process, she was a cheerleader, confidant, and resource. Her positivity was infectious, and her confidence in me humbling at times. I do not think she will ever know much her conviction helped me to stay the course. It is a rarity to find someone who loves a team as themselves, and this is what you find when you work with or for her.

I originally planned to take parts of what these employees sent me about this *ESFJ* but decided I did not want to minimize any of their thoughts. I have worked with this person over the last 14 years and my experiences with her are consistent with everything they have said. Their descriptions of this *ESFJ* are what you would expect of this type. Some of the words that are used to describe *ESFJs* are: dedicated, loyal, cooperative, organized, tactful, sociable, and responsive. They have described an *ESFJ* very well.

ENFJ
(Support others with energy and creativity)

The person I will use for the *ENFJ* is my friend Zellie. He, my wife, children, and Abraham Lincoln are the only people I have referenced by name. Zellie and I had an agreement that we could tell MBTI stories about each other anytime if they were fairly accurate and not embellished too much, which is not unusual for our types.

During the 30 years of our friendship and working together, we spent a great deal of time exploring how to help ourselves and others understand each other in a way which would improve our relationships and ability to accomplish the important things in life. We tried every tool we used before using it with others. We would examine those tools in the context of our lives first to see if it had value for us. Since we both used MBTI extensively, it was something we were constantly applying to ourselves. Zellie and I explored MBTI on a personal level in a variety of situations.

If there are degrees of *Extroversion*, Zellie was one of the most extraverted people I have ever known. In fact, on one MBTI assessment he took, he answered every *E/I* question like an *Extrovert* would. He used that *Extraversion* to engage people as effectively as anyone I have ever known. When you combined his *E* with *Feeling*, you had someone who loved to get to know and be with people. When we would travel to locations to do retreats or workshops, he would be friends with every receptionist, bellboy, and employee of the facility.

In his work and personal life, you saw the *EF* expressed in an active involvement in activities improving the quality of people's lives. He was instrumental in the building of an 8-mile scenic greenbelt walking and biking trail in our community. He helped design and build a ropes course for an area Boy Scout camp. He engaged a group of people to build and place blue bird houses in the area to make our community a bird sanctuary. He served as a facilitator for other community and church efforts. He was the ultimate "Energizer Bunny."

A good career match for an *ENFJ* is a corporate trainer and Zellie was the best I ever saw. He was an excellent class-room instructor, but his real strength as a trainer was the creativity associated with his *Intuition*. He loved experiential learning where he could take an activity which was fun and use it to teach a concept in a manner which enabled people to learn and apply what they had learned much more effectively than if they had attended a lecture.

Intuition was an important strength when he was lead facilitator for three consecutive Officers" retreats. Those retreats occurred every two years over a four-year period after Company A was divested from a larger company. After divestiture, Company A had approximately 14,000 employees and $4 billion in sales. The CEO was using the Officers' retreats to prepare the organization for a significant period of change. The company had to move from a large division of one of the largest and most recognized companies in the world to a much smaller independent company which would be competing with large companies in their business sector.

Zellie and other members of a planning team engaged with prominent external consultants and major business schools to plan these retreats with very strategic and transformational objectives. The activities and simulations had to drive home new ways of thinking which would prepare the organization for major new business challenges. His creativity was critical. The philosophy of "let's change it" associated with his combination of *EN* was a great match for the *EN* of the CEO.

One characteristic which contributed to some incredible accomplishments of Zellie was his idealism. He pursued lofty goals. This along with his *NJ* combination created a drive which at times became burdensome for him. He had such a passion for tackling challenges with real merit, and his *N* caused him, at times, to tackle unrealistic challenges. His *J* would push him beyond reasonable limits at times. He achieved so much more than most people, but he was always pushing for more. The tension of not always being able to complete the abundance of things he pursued was a challenge.

On an Officer's retreat one time, I was taking a walk with one of Company A's VPs after an activity and discussion Zellie had facilitated. The conversation surfaced some critical issues which many people would normally avoid. The VP and I were discussing how important the interactions were and how unusual these discussions were in most companies. The VP shared this insight: "Rick, the reason people were willing to discuss those sensitive issues is because Zellie is the most non-threatening person they know." That was so true and the caring, loyalty, and supportiveness which are characteristic of the *ENFJ* made this quite natural for Zellie.

ENTJ
(Take charge and take logical, decisive action)

The example I will use to illustrate an *ENTJ* is the previous CEO for Company B. It is not unusual for a CEO to be an *ENTJ*. One phrase used to describe *ENTJs* is "they are born with combat booties." Put a hill in front of them and they are ready to lead the charge. They love a challenge and attack the challenge with a controlled tough-mindedness.

When this *ENTJ* took over the leadership of Company B twenty-three years ago, it was a part of Company A. Company A was downsizing in the U.S. locations where Company B had locations and Company B only served employees and family members of Company A. As a result, in a highly competitive business where size helps you be competitive, Company B was facing a gradually decreasing member base for the future.

This was a perfect hill for this new *ENTJ* CEO to attack. Over the first four years in his role as CEO, he led the organization to spin off from Company A and become an independent financial institution. They also changed their charter from a company charter to one which enabled them to serve people who were not employees of Company A in the communities they served. Over his 22 years as CEO, he would lead Company B to significant growth as indicated by: increasing their membership, assets, and number of employees by a factor of seven and growing from 8 to 29 branches.

While achieving this growth, Company B performed in the top forty-three on the ten measures used in their business sector for benchmarking against their 5,700 plus peers. They were top fourteen in half of those measures. You combine this type of performance with unparalleled scores on satisfaction from the members they serve, and you get a sense of the type of organization Company B has become.

This type of business performance is consistent with the *ENTJ* type. The two areas which really stand out to me about this leader relates to the way he has used MBTI to improve his personal effectiveness. While he was the CEO, he would come to talk with each of the leadership classes. He would emphasize the importance of their role in leading the employees of Company B. He would also discuss ways he has used MBTI over the years in his role as a leader.

One area he would discuss, and I saw him apply at times, was making sure his *N* did not push too much on the organization in a way which would distract them in their role of serving the member and promoting growth, which were two major goals of Company B. I took suggestions to him often which I thought had merit to pursue. On most occasions, his response was something like this: "Rick, that's an interesting idea, however, at this time our employees have a lot on their plate, and I don't want to cause them to lose focus." He was great at recognizing the value in being able to prioritize from a list of great ideas.

The final thing he was able to do that is not always evident with *ENTJs* is to consider the impact of decisions and actions upon people. *ENTJs* are so ready to lead you into a battle they at times forget the impact of these actions upon the people they are leading. This *ENTJ* learned early in his career how important it is to weigh the human factor and he became extremely effective in doing so. In addition, he led Company B to make it a deeply rooted value in the organizational culture.

Here is part of a note he sent to his Senior Leadership Team after the annual Management Council meeting for all managers in the organization the year prior to his retirement:

"You guys reinforced that caring and concern for others, empathy, honesty, humor, respect for others, kindness, and dare I say it 'LOVE' are a big part of how our company is different. Those elements are now a core part of our culture (because Senior Management Team has consistently modeled those behaviors for many years) and I have always believed those same characteristics really drive a big part of our overall success especially in our relations with each other, staff, members, and the board. It really comes out in our relationship with each other and all employees, our success with member service and our support for communities and our branding of who we really are to the public. I am proud we have a caring organization at Company B, which has also been wildly successful by any business standard. What a wonderful outcome reinforcing again where Company B has chosen to be different frequently drives a lot of our success."

This former CEO used the natural strengths associated with an *ENTJ* beautifully through his 22 years in that role. The thing that impressed me most was how he utilized MBTI and other feedback to use his lesser preferred preferences in a way which contributed to his personal success and the success and growth of an organization impacting thousands of lives in a positive way.

- **What:** The four-letter MBTI type provides a comprehensive and helpful model for understanding the way we prefer to function in our everyday world.

- **So What:** By understanding our own and the type of others, we can better appreciate the totality of who we are.
- **Now What:** I can use my understanding of type to better play to my strengths and develop in areas I struggle. I can also use an understanding of another person's type to improve my relationship with them by considering their natural behavioral preferences.

CLOSING

This book has been floating around in my head for years and it has been such a joy to get it out. When you have benefited from something in your life, and you have also seen hundreds of situations where it has benefited others, you want to share it. This is the reason I authored this book. It is not about how much I know. It is much more about how much I have seen.

I hope you have enjoyed the stories. More importantly, I hope you have gained something from them which will help you better understand yourself and others.

I love the MBTI and I have not sought to sell it, but to explore it in a way to help you see how useful it is as a framework for understanding human behavior. I hope it becomes a helpful tool for you as it has been for me.

I am writing this amidst the tragic death of George Floyd and massive protests and violent demonstrations fueled by the anger related to the way his life was taken. These types of events in our lives demonstrate the absolute urgency and critical importance of our understanding one another. We can never build caring and just relationships without understanding. If this book has helped you better understand others in your life, I will be satisfied.

Thanks for taking your time to read my thoughts.

ACKNOWLEDGMENTS

My foundation for an understanding of psychology and psychological tools like the Myers-Briggs Type Indicator (MBTI) was built in my doctoral program in educational and counseling psychology at the University of Tennessee. I learned the power of these tools to help individuals and groups grow, develop, make good decisions, and take actions to improve their lives. I am indebted to my professors who prepared me to use the MBTI in counseling and educational settings.

BIBLIOGRAPHY

Dunning, Donna, (2003). *Introduction to Type and Communication.* Mountain View, CA. Consulting Psychologists Press, Inc.

Hirsh, Elizabeth, Hirsh, Katherine and Hirsh, Sandra Krebs, (2002). *Introduction to Type and Teams 2nd Edition.* Mountain View, CA. Consulting Psychologists Press, Inc.

Hirsh, Sandra Krebs and Kummerow, Jean M. (1998). *Introduction to Type in Organizations.* Consulting Psychologist Press, Inc.

Keirsey, David, and Bates, Marilyn, (1984). *Please Understand Me: Character and Temperament Types.* Del Mar, CA. Prometheus Nemesis Book Company; 5th edition.

Lawrence, G. (1982). *People Types and Tiger Stripes.* Gainesville, FL: Center for Applications of Psychological Type

Myers, I. B. (1980), *Introduction to type (3rd ed.).* Palo Alto, CA: Consulting Psychologists Press, Inc.

ABOUT THE AUTHOR

Rick Toomey's life has provided him with a rich variety of educational, work, and life experiences. His clear preference for *Perceiving* has resulted in a curiosity about people and a life driven by a passion for understanding and appreciating a wide variety of people, interests, and perspectives.

His higher education started with a B.S. in Industrial Management from the University of Tennessee. This provided a great foundation for understanding how organizations worked to accomplish their missions. He then completed a master's degree in the field of Religious Education, from Southern Baptist Theological Seminary, which prepared him to help others learn with a strong focus on the spiritual dimension of life. Finally, he completed an Ed.D. in Educational and Counseling Psychology from the University of Tennessee which helped him to better understand people and how to enable them to address important life issues.

His work experiences have included working as a minister, counselor, manager, corporate trainer, organizational development consultant, and assistant college professor. Much of his work experience was with two major companies who are described as Company A and Company B in this book. Both of those companies provided opportunities to learn and grow through work experiences and his work associates.

His life experiences include his dear wife, Marcie, two wonderful children, Kelly and Chris, and other family members and friends.

Living all aspects of life with them has provided a marvelous crucible for learning the importance of understanding.

This book would not have been possible without professors like Dr. Dietz, Dr. Gordon, Dr. Stagg, Dr. Hinson, Dr. Oates, Dr. DeRidder, and more. Work associates who have taught and applied MBTI so well provided the real substance of this book, and he is so indebted to people like Zellie, Carol, Olan, Allan, Raj, Kelly, Ken, Jerry, Fielding, and others.

The most important contributors to this author are the 2,000 plus people and over a hundred teams who provided the author with wonderful learning experiences which enabled him to gain a deeper understanding of MBTI and how to apply the concepts to improving personal effectiveness and achievement of life goals. Thanks to each of them.

Rick Toomey is currently working on a book with a co-author entitled, *Neither Jew Nor Greek*, in which they explore their personal journey in relation to racism and the influence of Christianity on beliefs about racism.

CPSIA information can be obtained
at www.ICGtesting.com
Printed in the USA
JSHW011910081022
31396JS00001B/2